The
SMART RUNNER'S HANDBOOK

YOUR PASSPORT TO GREAT RUNNING!

ABOUT THE AUTHOR

Matt Greenwald has been a competitive runner for more than fifteen years. He has designed running programs for many friends over the years, and this book is the culmination of all his training ideas and advice. Matt currently lives in Washington, DC, where he works as a professional staff member for the US Senate Budget Committee.

ACKNOWLEDGMENTS

I would like to thank the many people who made this book possible. I'll start with my father, the former sports editor of the *Daily Pennsylvanian*, who provided numerous helpful editing suggestions, not to mention a strong dose of guidance and confidence throughout my life. My mother, for always being there during the rough days early on in my running career. To all my college cross country teammates, who made those years the most enjoyable period of my running life. My good friend and high school cross country captain, Paul Guastadesigni, his guidance and achievement provided me the inspiration I needed to overcome the difficulties I faced during my early running days.

I would also like to thank the following for their contributions to the book: Jose Blanco, Andy Liss, Sarah Hubbard for their great work in posing for the cover. Sue Ellen Hopkinson, Alex "Deek" Indorf, Michael Regan, Marty Langelan, and the American Running and Fitness Association.

Finally, I would like to thank Jonathan Stein, for showing a willingness to make this book a reality.

The

SMART RUNNER'S HANDBOOK

YOUR PASSPORT TO GREAT RUNNING!

MATT GREENWALD

OPEN ROAD PUBLISHING

OPEN ROAD PUBLISHING

We offer travel guides to American and foreign locales. Our books tell it like it is, often with an opinionated edge, and our experienced authors always give you all the information you need to have the trip of a lifetime. Write for your free catalog of all our titles, including our golf and restaurant guides.

Catalog Department, Open Road Publishing
P.O. Box 20226, Columbus Circle Station, New York, NY 10023

Or you can contact us by e-mail at:
Jopenroad@aol.com

2nd Edition

For
GBG, BJG and Lidie L.

Disclaimer: As with any physical fitness book, you need to exercise common sense and take into account your physical condition before you start any running program. For pregnant women in particular, please consult your doctor.

TABLE OF CONTENTS

SIDEBARS

1. INTRODUCTION

You too can have a superior running program! Improve your time, be better prepared, minimize the risk of problems or injuries – and have more fun out there no matter what your ability. Once you've finished this book, you'll be a better runner, a healthier runner, a *smarter* runner.

I'm going to show you everything you need to know to design a running program that's best suited to your needs. We'll go over speed workouts, diet, equipment and gear, mental preparation, and race training strategies for different levels and abilities. Whether you're a beginner planning on running a 10K, an intermediate or advanced runner striving to do better in a marathon, or are simply looking for more enjoyment and endurance, you'll find it all in this book.

Each of the main ideas developed here are illustrated with three examples from runners at different stages of ability and skill. Each example magnifies common problems and offers appropriate solutions. I offer a range of possibilities, but more importantly I'll help you figure out which is the best way to go in diverse situations.

Why work out your own program? Because if you just get out there and start running without any forethought – even if you've been running for years – you'll get off on the wrong foot and will surely develop difficulties that may be hard to overcome. A smart runner has a plan, one that's easy to design and will produce results. Devoting some up-front time and energy to the concepts I've developed in this book will ensure that you'll get far more out of your running than if you just grab your gear and head to the track. It's worked for me, and I know it can work for you.

I've also included a chapter on the special needs of women runners and running during pregnancy, based on extensive study and working with a variety of women runners to set up the best possible programs. Many of my friends have already benefited from the advice I've collected in these areas, and I'm pleased to include them in this book.

So get out there and hit the pavement, but do it right, and do it smart – with **THE SMART RUNNER'S HANDBOOK**.

2. FIVE BASIC PRINCIPLES FOR SUCCESS

KEEP THE FAITH

Most of us endure a love-hate relationship with the sport of running. Across all levels of ability, from the serious marathoner to the runner who is just trying to get in a few miles every other day or so, we all experience the highs and lows of running. Many times both sensations are felt during a single run.

The downside of running includes the tightness in our leg muscles that we often experience for the first five to ten minutes of a run. On the really tough days, it feels as if the World Trade Center Towers are attached to our legs. Other times, it's not just our legs but our entire bodies that suffer.

Then there's inertia. It can strike after a tiring day of work, or during the middle of a stubborn cold. One part of our mind tells us to get out there and run, while the other tries to talk us into hitting the couch for a pre-dinner cocktail or snack in front of the T.V. After much procrastination, we put on the running shoes and hit the pavement. During the beginning of the run, when it feels like someone is draining a pint of blood from our bodies during each stride, we wonder whether it's all worth it.

Is it worth it? Of course it is – as long as you're willing to show enough persistence to overcome those difficult moments. Remember, the positive rewards that lie ahead last far longer. As time goes by, the tough periods become shorter and easier to handle. The struggle encountered at the start or finish of a run becomes shorter. One lousy day is followed by four strong outings. Instead of dwelling on the negative, you begin to appreciate all the positive, healthy aspects running has to offer to both your mind and body.

One of the many benefits of running that I particularly value is how it relaxes your mind. Many runners experience a calm, satisfying feeling during and after a run. Running has been credited with triggering the release in the brain of the morphine-like hormone known as beta-endorphin, which may account for what many call a "runners high." Personally, the mental benefits I have derived from running turned me into a productive student during my college and graduate school days. More recently, running has enhanced my performance in the workplace.

There's far too much to gain from running to let an off day or a few bad moments keep you from moving forward.

PREPARE FOR YOUR RUN

Smart runners know that preparation is a key to success. Your performance hinges on factors beyond the effort you put in during a run. Many other variables such as your diet, sleeping habits, participation in other sports, the value you place on stretching, the running shoes you select, etc. also play a role in determining how well you will run. You're not going to get that far running on five hours of sleep, wearing a pair of basketball shoes and eating a Big Mac with fries an hour before a run. You should consider the impact some of your routine activities will have on your running. Attempt to also devote time and effort to ensuring that you start out your run in the best possible condition.

I'm not suggesting you must transform yourself into a tofu eating, carrot juice drinking vegetarian who stretches all day at her desk and goes to bed at 9:30 in order to wake up at 5:30 A.M. to eat granola and do yoga. However, there a few less arduous things you can do to ensure that you run at your full potential.

They include getting in a minimum of seven hours of sleep a night, buying decent running shoes, stretching for 5-10 minutes before and after a run, giving yourself four hours to digest a full meal before running and drinking plenty of water before heading out on hot days. It makes sense to set yourself up for the best run possible.

A CHANGE OF SCENERY ALWAYS HELPS

Showing some creativity about your running location serves to enhance your experience. Far too many runners fall into the habit of not adding enough variety in choosing their run.

Incorporating **multiple routes** in your running routine is important for three basic reasons. First, it helps to lower the probability of injury. Second, it keeps your motivational level up. Third, it enables you to simultaneously build up both your speed and endurance.

Having access to a route at least once a week where the terrain is primarily made up of grass or dirt will significantly reduce the possibility of suffering a serious injury. It's a good idea to give your leg muscles, joints, ligaments, and tendons an occasional break from the constant pounding of running on hard pavement.

Developing multiple routes is also a simple way to make running more interesting. It's a lot easier to keep yourself motivated to get out there every day if you know you will not be running past the same sights, sounds, hills, or long boring stretches as the day before. Personally, I try to avoid running the same route more than once a week.

Finally, alternating your runs between primarily hilly and flat terrain enables you to work on both your endurance and speed. The runs consisting of numerous hills offer a great opportunity to improve your stamina. A generally flat course gives you the chance to focus more on speed. The long straightaways offer you the opportunity to throw in some up-tempo surges.

Many of you may not have much control over where you are able to run. Those who live in the center of large cities are often limited to one park or a route along a river. Others who run at work are usually confined by time and an urban environment. Those of you new to running, as well as others who are not in the best of shape, are constrained by the limited amount of distance you're able to run.

Even if you fall into the above categories, it's still possible to add a little diversity to your runs. At least remember to reverse the direction of your run, especially if your run involves numerous loops around a small area. Changing direction is a simple way to make a run more interesting to complete. I'm always amazed at how different the same route seems just by running it in reverse. In the case of runs consisting of many loops or turns, changing direction serves to balance the strain on the lower part of whichever leg is on the inside during the turns.

Running at work offers you the opportunity to run with a partner. This usually makes the run more enjoyable and the time go by faster. I often push myself harder when I run with other people, and you probably will too.

So instead of wasting time searching for excuses, keep on lacing up those running shoes and get out there and run!

FINDING YOUR OWN COMFORT LEVEL

Running is more individually-oriented than just about any other sport. Far too many runners at all levels of ability are inclined to base their training too rigidly on what successful runners are doing. What works well for someone else may or may not work for you. Runners of similar ability frequently take different paths towards achieving the same goal.

Take the example of two runners who are capable of running a 10-K in the same time. They both may even run the same amount of miles a week, say 30 miles. But how they get to 30 miles for the week varies considerably. One of them finds that she is more effective if she takes two days off a week. The other runner only needs one day off or none at all. The first runner benefits from doing a speed workout once a week. The other responds more favorably to a long run on the weekend.

I'm not suggesting that you should ignore advice offered by other runners. Putting together a solid training program based on the experience of others will often help you achieve positive results. Just keep in mind that no two runners are the same. To varying degrees, we all respond differently to the same training regimen.

Be extra careful about seeking advice from those talented runners blessed with large doses of natural ability. Many excellent runners give lousy advice to other runners. They have a habit of forgetting how much effort it takes to reach a level where your stomach stops sounding like a washing machine and your legs no longer feel like lead. It's analogous to the plight of the of Hall of Fame baseball players who decide to take up managing or coaching. Most of them make lousy managers and coaches, because they are unable to instruct at a level useful to the average major league ballplayer.

Whether you are a beginner to the sport, or an experienced runner hoping to rise to the next level, it's important to start out training at a comfortable level. (You'll have plenty of opportunities to test your mettle down the road.) First and foremost, listen to what your body tells you. How your body is responding to your training is the best indicator of whether you are getting the most out of your runs. Ultimately, your body becomes your best and most valuable coach.

Those of you new to the sport frequently experience soreness in your leg muscles and shins during the first couple of weeks of running. If the discomfort continues to persist, you might want to consider taking an extra day off or shortening some runs until you feel better. Many experienced runners often begin to feel a bit worn down as they take on a heavier training schedule in the hope of improving their time. In this case, their body is probably sending the signal to increase the intensity of training at a more gradual pace.

Being cautious in responding to your body's aches and pains does not give you the liberty to use a slight feeling of fatigue or tightness in your legs as an excuse for not sticking to the planned run for the day. At all levels of running, it is important to remain motivated enough prior to and at the beginning of a run to believe you will complete the run as planned. Equally vital is the ability to show enough flexibility to modify your workout, slightly or more radically, based on how you feel once you get into the run. The beginning of a run can frequently be the most difficult part, and it is not the basis for gauging how well you are feeling on a particular day.

STRIVE FOR CONSISTENCY

Striking the proper balance between pushing yourself enough to keep pace with a challenging training schedule and giving your body enough of a cushion to adjust to that schedule is important. Reaching that happy medium is the key to maintaining a level of **consistency** in your training. Consistency enables you to raise both the quantity and the quality of your running. It provides a sturdy underpinning on which to build your running skills.

This solid base is established by developing the ability over a period of weeks — or even months — of sticking to a standard training schedule. The trick is being able to do it without feeling pushed to the limit physically or mentally. For the novice runner, it means getting used to being out there three or four times a week and putting in two to four miles a run. For a more advanced runner, it translates into getting accustomed to running six to seven days a week and maintaining a weekly average of twenty-five to fifty miles depending on your level of ability.

Whatever your level, developing a consistent routine will make it easier for you to get through the rough days. Being able to successfully complete rough days is important. It makes the future down days easier to get through, and increases the likelihood you will bounce back on the next day with a strong run.

Making the adjustment to a consistent training schedule is not easy at first. Over time, however, as long as you stay determined and show some discipline, the entire process will run smoother (no pun intended). Keep in mind that each time you are able to get over the hump mentally by not quitting on a day when you don't feel so great, you are strengthening yourself. The physical gain is the obvious by-product of choosing to keep on running rather than walking. One reinforces the other. The combination of mental confidence and the physical benefits that flow from following through on these runs reduces the amount of off days you'll experience in the future. This makes it a whole lot easier to remain consistent with your overall training schedule.

3. WEATHER & RUNNING ATTIRE

Far too many runners allow imperfect weather conditions determine their training. While it's difficult to find ways to compensate for extreme weather conditions, most of what you face day in and day out should not dramatically alter your planned workout schedule. In fact, when properly prepared, running in poor weather conditions can actually serve to enhance your training. There is a lot to be said for not letting Mother Nature get the best of you.

RUNNING IN COLD WEATHER

In many parts of the country, **cold weather** offers a great opportunity to get in months of solid endurance-building running. It probably has to do with all the years I spent running in New England during my college days, but there are few sensations that beat the feeling of being loose and warmed up after some outdoor athletic activity on a brisk, cold day.

The good thing about cold weather (except in the case of extreme conditions) is that you can always compensate for the temperature by dressing up. Granted, there are some days in the winter, especially in the upper portions of the Midwest and Northeast, where no amount of speciality running attire is going to help fend off the cold. But most of us don't have to contend with sub-zero weather and wind chills registering in the negative 20 to 30 degree range.

Dress for Success!

Generally, when dressing for the cold, wear more on top than on your legs. Don't make the mistake of thinking that because your legs are so important they need more protection from the cold. The parts of your body that need the most protection are the areas that you use the least when running. Obviously, your legs are not one of these parts.

The fact that your legs are constantly in motion while you run means they represent the easiest part of your body to warm up. Why bog them down with too much garb? It's your head and upper body that need the most shielding from the cold.

COLD WEATHER LEG GEAR

I don't cover up my legs unless the temperature is under 45 degrees. In college, I would not be caught dead running in a pair of running tights. I have since gotten over that insecurity and use lycra running tights all the time during the winter. Happily, manufacturers have come out with more loose fitting forms of tights that work just about as well. Various styles of tights are available at most sporting goods or running stores. Running tights are far lighter in weight and less bulky than either nylon or cotton sweat pants, and keep your legs warmer. They also are far less expensive than the more fancy Gortex running pants, which, except under the most extreme conditions, will cause you to sweat almost uncontrollably.

It's only when the temperature falls below 20 degrees, accompanied with a serious wind chill, that I put a pair of nylon sweat pants over my tights. I never use cotton sweat pants when I run. They are heavier and offer less warmth – the wind goes right through them – than tights, Gortex or nylon.

For the top part of your body, I suggest using layers of thin clothing rather than wearing loose and heavy sweatshirts or jackets. Many runners have the habit of panicking in the cold weather and overdressing. Layering gives you the option of gradually stripping down during a run if you begin to feel too warm. The inner layers of clothing should be the thinnest and fit the tightest. A popular fabric to use for the inner layer is **polypropylene**. It's a light and flexible material that breathes well, allowing moisture to escape. Shirts made of polypropylene and other similar fabrics can be purchased at any running or athletic specialty store.

The outer layer should fit more loosely for two reasons. A tight fit will restrict both your stride and the ability of your inner layer to breathe. For the outer layer, try nylon or other types of wind-resistant fabrics that are well ventilated. Using a Gortex running top, the popular and expensive choice of many winter runners, can be overkill, except in the case of severe cold weather. Running in Gortex can cause you to sweat beyond a comfortable level, especially if you run a minute-per-mile clip of under eight minutes.

I'm not suggesting that buying a Gortex top is always a waste of money. The manufacturers of running jackets have recently come out with lighter versions of Gortex tops that wear better in less extreme cold conditions. In the past, the serious runner was forced to buy separate jackets for the rain and cold weather. Many of the new lightweight models now on the market can be used to protect yourself from both the spring rain and winter wind.

Many runners, myself included, have gone out and purchased one of those terrific wind-resistant, insulated, and ventilated running jackets, only to make the mistake of wearing an all cotton T-shirt underneath. The problem is that under extreme weather conditions cotton absorbs all your sweat and keeps the moisture close to your body. Don't settle for just getting one layer of clothing right.

I'm not suggesting that you give up wearing all those old comfortable cotton T-shirts and purchase several high-tech fabric shirts manufactured by the nation's leading chemical companies. On days when the temperature is in the low forties, I'll still opt for a long sleeve cotton T-shirt and a thin sweatshirt. It's only under more severe weather conditions, both hot and cold, that I make an effort to change some of my old habits and take advantage of what the new high-tech running age has to offer.

The most important parts of your body to keep warm when running in cold weather are your hands and head. Wearing a wool hat and gloves can make a big difference. The gloves don't have to be anything fancy. I usually wear a cheap pair of gardening gloves. In the past, I have also used socks, which work well, since they allow me to continuously rub my fingers together in order to keep them warm.

Try to avoid wearing gloves or using socks that are made of cotton. It tends to act like a sponge, causing your gloves to become drenched in sweat. Wearing a hat that at least partially covers your ears is a good idea. We lose close to 80 percent of the heat in our bodies through our heads. I opt for the hat and gloves once the temperature dips below 40 degrees.

Cold Weather Pro's & Con's
Once you are properly attired — layers on top and light on the legs — the cold weather offers an excellent training environment. Unlike hot weather, in which it is harder to compensate for the heat, running conditions in the winter months frequently don't vary much from the more ideal spring and fall seasons.

It may take an extra five to ten minutes to loosen up, but then you can stay warmed up without the danger of becoming overheated later in the run. The sun and heat, two of the most destructive forces runners face, are neutralized in the cold weather. This gives you more energy to apply to the middle and end parts of your runs. In fact, during the winter months you will be more likely to finish your runs stronger.

Dealing with Cold Weather Elements
I'm not suggesting that the entire winter season is a paradise for training. There are three elements of nature associated with the cold that frequently wreak havoc on runners: **wind**, **snow**, and **ice**.

As the mercury in the thermometer falls below 40 degrees, the **wind** begins to be a factor during your runs. There isn't much you can do to protect yourself from it. As mentioned previously, purchasing a Gortex running top and avoiding the use of cotton sweat pants can help. For the most part, however, you just have to grit your teeth and bear it. Be sure to cover up your ears, and I even go as far as wearing a bandanna around my neck.

WHAT TO EXPOSE!

The only parts of your body that should be directly exposed to a strong wind are your nose, cheeks, and mouth. Some runners even resort to using ski masks, but I find that as long as I have my ears and the top of my head covered, I'm usually alright.

For the most part, **snow** is an inconvenience to runners, not an insurmountable problem. Until the stuff is cleared off the streets and shoveled on the sidewalks, it can turn many routes into an obstacle course. Even after it's cleared, you are likely to find yourself having to hurdle over or running around many small snow banks. Try to keep the jumping around to a minimum. The landings put needless added pressure on your legs, increasing the risk of injury, especially in cold weather when your muscles are less likely to be warmed up.

There is a positive side to snow, beyond its aesthetic benefit, once it becomes packed down. It transforms the sidewalk or street into a softer surface to run on, much like a dirt trail. This reduces the pounding absorbed by leg muscles and joints.

I consider **ice** to be the most serious threat to maintaining a consistent training schedule over the winter months. The lack of sure footing can produce a number of harmful effects. First, it hampers your form. You feel inclined to **soft step** over icy patches of sidewalks and streets in order to remain sure footed. You run slower and fall out of sync with your normal stride.

Second, there's always that fear of falling on your face. There is no easy solution to this problem. I have not found any technique that keeps me confident about not slipping and or falling.

When faced with ice, curl your toes in an effort to get better traction, and try to land further up on the balls of your feet to keep your motion going forward. That way if you do slip, you're more likely to fall forward than on your back.

The final danger of ice is the heightened risk of others interfering with your run. Cars are the biggest concern. I do not run on the street if conditions are bad. It's tempting to hit the streets, which, as a result of traffic and salt trucks, are usually in better shape than sidewalks following an ice or sleet storm. But stick to the sidewalks and avoid the risk of having to contend with skidding cars suddenly attempting to get out of your way.

ICE HASSLES: DON'T SUCCUMB TO THE "MOTHER TECHNIQUE!"

*When running on ice, don't resort to what I call the **mother technique** for dealing with ice. My mother has a habit of instantly transforming herself into a toddler just learning to take her first steps when she is faced with walking on ice. That's not all that changes. Mentally, she becomes more uptight, forgetting her normally sweet disposition. As a result, she makes a tricky situation worse by letting herself get so psyched out.*

Considering all the wonderful things my mom has done for our family, she has earned the right to use the "mother technique" as often as she wishes. We'll even wait for her. For the rest of us, try not to make a slippery situation worse by over-compensating too much.

DEALING WITH HEAT

The single toughest outside variable runners have to contend with is the **heat.** You can always throw on another layer of clothing when it gets colder, but there is only so much you can do to compensate when running in hot weather.

The danger zone for experiencing some sort of heat-related complication usually starts once the temperature rises above the low seventies, with a humidity reading of over fifty percent.

However, there is not any absolute combination of temperature and humidity threshold that applies to all runners. The risk of suffering from heat exhaustion also depends on the distance you plan to run and the shape you are in. But once the temperature starts hovering around ninety degrees or greater, all runners, no matter what shape they are in or the distance they are running, must take precautions.

The best weapon to use against the heat is **water**. Drink plenty of water during the hours leading up to your run, but try to avoid gulping down more than one full glass within the thirty minutes before going out. The heat will be tough enough to deal with – don't make the situation worse by adding cramps to the run by drinking too much water prior to your run.

DRINKING ON THE RUN

If you are running more than just a few miles on an exceedingly hot day, don't hesitate to stop at least once for a brief water break. Some people like to run with water bottles attached to a belt. These can be purchased at most running/athletic stores. That's fine as long as you do not find the belt to be too cumbersome. A more common practice is choosing a route where you will pass a working water fountain. These are easy to find in most parks. If your run involves more than one loop, another option is to make a quick stop at your house.

Besides down your throat, the second most important area to apply water is on the back of your neck. The area behind your neck is the most efficient cooling connecting point to the rest of your body. A cup of water splashed behind your neck, or better yet, a wet cold sponge, can go a long way on a hot day's run.

Water makes up one important part of the equation for fighting the heat. Another is **using your mind**. In order to encourage friends to run on hot days, I tell them to think of it as an opportunity to get in two runs for the price of one. Going out and running five miles on an 85 degree day involves more of an effort than running five on a 65 degree day. The extra effort also has the benefits of leaving your body in better shape than it would be from doing the run under more favorable conditions. Therefore, you're getting more bang for the buck. In running terms, it means achieving greater endurance capabilities without having to increase your mileage.

Using your mind means keeping focused on the positive aspects that result from training in hot weather, rather than letting yourself get intimidated by what it takes to achieve results. For example, race times in 10-Ks and marathons for dedicated runners at all levels are usually lower in the fall than in the spring.

Smart runners reap the benefit of sticking to a solid training schedule during the hot summer months. Instead of letting yourself get all worked up by the heat before you even hit the pavement, consider it as a terrific opportunity to raise the quality of your training.

Running in the Rain

Rain can work for you in a similar manner. Far too many people get psyched out about running in the rain. If a long hard run is scheduled during a downpour, many people will put it off for another day.

But rain can be an excellent source of diversion. Usually when running in heavy rain, you end up concentrating so much on the rain that you forget how hard you are running. You are too preoccupied with the rain to worry about how tired you are becoming from putting in such a strong effort. On a hot day, rain will also cool you down on your run.

Dressing for the Heat

There's little you can do to protect yourself from the heat in terms of choosing **what to wear**. One common mistake many runners make is still opting for their favorite all cotton T-shirts when running in the heat. It's a frequent blunder runners make, and easy to understand given how comfortable cotton feels against the skin. But the truth is cotton absorbs moisture like a sponge. It does not allow the heat and moisture to escape your body nearly as much as other materials.

Polyester and **nylon-based fabrics** breathe and stay much dryer than cotton. Manufacturers of running clothes have made significant improvements in making polyester-based fabrics more comfortable to the skin. These materials do not shrink when washed. On most hot days, you are still likely to prefer to put on one of your time-tested, well-worn cotton t-shirts. I know I still do. But on those really hot days, you may want to switch to a polyester or nylon fabric.

Once the temperature rises into the 90's, any bravado about taking on the hot weather with gusto should be toned down and re-thought. Serious risks to your health, such as heat exhaustion, dehydration, and even heart failure can result from over-extending yourself during extreme heat conditions. Those with a good deal of experience with running in the heat, and have no history of heart problems, are at less risk. But all runners must recognize that when the thermometer starts to rise above the unbearable level, common sense dictates caution.

At the end of my first marathon, at a time when I was in the best shape of my life, I almost collapsed from heat exhaustion. I made the mistake of showing my lack of deference to the heat by not stopping often enough for water.

RUNNING SHOES

It seems that every time I become comfortable with a particular pair of running shoes, the sneaker company that made them decides to discontinue production of that shoe. Usually, they will come out with a "new and improved" version changing the colors, the style name, and of course, the price tag by about $20. Other than that, not much else changes. The shoe companies do not make it easy for you to stick with the time-proven adage: if it ain't broke, don't fix it. There are a few classic models, such as Nike's *Pegasus*, that have stood the test of time.

More important than the shoes you choose to run in is how often you replace them. Running in the latest top-of-the-line $120 model is not going to offer you much of an advantage over the more modestly priced versions if you continue to use them once they are worn out. In fact, continuing to run in worn out shoes that need to be replaced is one of the leading causes of injuries. It's far wiser to buy a pair of sneakers in the mid-price range of $60 to $85 and replace it every six months or 400-500 miles of running, than to purchase a super-expensive model and run in them for an entire year. In fact, most shoe manufacturers offer their best product lines in the moderate price range. There are exceptions to this rule. Heavier runners may have to pay more for special motion control features.

Often it is possible to tell when a running shoe needs to be replaced by looking at the condition of the outer and mid-soles. But let me add a word of caution. Shoes have become so technologically advanced that it's becoming more difficult to discover the wear by just looking at them. Many shoes today compress long before they show any hint of wear on the outer or mid-sole. Also, listen to your body. Unusual soreness in your leg muscles may signal it's time to buy a new pair of running shoes.

The outer sole, usually black, is where the traction design resides. Usually, after a few months of training, the traction pattern begins to wear thin and get uneven. The mid-sole is the portion of the shoe connecting the outer sole to the part of the shoe containing your foot. The make-up consists usually of some sort of foam or rubbery cushion.

After a period of time, the mid-sole will start to compress, and frequently will begin to wear unevenly above the heel. A compressed mid-sole offers less of a cushion to your legs and no longer absorbs the shock from the constant pounding that results from running. Uneven wear of either the mid-sole or the outer sole causes an imbalance in your weight distribution while running. This results in the wrong parts of your legs absorbing too large a share of the burden, which raises the risk of injury.

Go to a store that caters specifically to runners rather than the many sneaker store chains. The sales people at running stores usually are experienced runners. They are able to provide more personalized service. Bring in your old running shoes and ask the salesperson to evaluate the wear of the mid-sole and outer sole. Who better to understand the needs of a runner than another runner?

Prices at the major sneaker chains and sporting goods stores usually aren't any lower than running stores, and most of their salespeople offer little, if any, understanding of the issues important to runners. The only time I will purchase a shoe from these stores is when I know in advance what I want to buy, and they have it at a better price.

There is no one best shoe out there. Find the shoe that fits your feet the best. In the past, the major innovations took place in the mid and outer soles of the shoes. Today, the focus is on the shape of shoe. Manufacturers are now offering shoes custom made to fit the individual shapes of runner's feet. A wider range of widths is now available. Generally, shoes are designed to match three types of variations in the arch of the foot: flat, normal and high. Runners with flat arches have a habit of over-pronating, and need a shoe with a lot of stability and a strong heel counter. Cushioning and flexibility are the two things runners with high arches need the most.

WHAT BRAND SHOULD YOU BUY?

*Generally, **Nike** and **Reebok** shoes are designed for runners with narrow feet and high arches. **Asics** and **Adidas** most often accommodate those with normal sized feet. **New Balance, Brooks,** and **Saucony** make shoes with wider widths, which cater to the needs of flat-footed and heavier runners, many of whom have a tendency to **pronate** while they run. Pronation occurs when the pressure from striking on the heel of your foot causes your legs to rotate inwards. This puts added pressure on your knees and hips.*

There are a few important variables that must be considered before deciding on a particular shoe. One consideration is your **training goals**. Are you a high or low mileage runner? Another consideration is the kind of surface that you most often run on. Do you do most of your running on pavement, trails, or grass? Overall body size is also important. Anyone over 180 pounds should select a more rigid shoe providing more stability.

Most shoes run a quarter to a half size smaller than your normal foot size. Don't make the mistake of buying a shoe that feels too snug. Running shoes do not stretch out over time. They keep the same shape. The best time to buy shoes is in the late afternoon or evening when your feet tend to swell up a bit. Try not to get too caught up with the gimmicks many shoe manufactures like to highlight. It's far more important to find a shoe that feels comfortable than it is to dwell on the little extras like *Gel Air* or *Grip*.

It's hard to keep up with all the new models of running shoes. Two of the best guides for reviewing what's out there, old and new, are published annually by *Runner's World* and *Consumer Reports*. Women's Sports and Fitness provides updated reviews on the latest women's running shoes. These issues include prices, as well as whether each shoe meets various standards and purposes.

The best buys on running shoes are found in the middle price range. Most of you will not need the extras, which are often just gimmicks. The only exception is for heavier runners. They need many of the features that the more expensive shoes offer.

WOMEN'S RUNNING SHOES

*Shoe manufacturers are beginning to put greater emphasis on designing running shoes that take into consideration the special needs of **women runners**. Most women's feet are narrower in the heel and wider in the toe box relative to men. Make sure you get a comfortable fit.*

For those of you who do either speed workouts on a track or participate in road races on a regular basis, you may want to consider purchasing a second pair of lighter running shoes for these runs. Commonly referred to as **racing flats**, their lightweight and airy feeling offers you a slight edge on those days when you expect to run a little faster than usual.

But don't get into the habit of wearing racing flats on a semi-regular basis. They are not sturdy enough to be used for daily training purposes, and frequent use could result in leg injuries. Also, repeated use may cause you to lose the sense of feeling light on your feet relative to your customary running shoes.

If you frequently run on trails you may want to consider buying a second pair of running shoes. A shoe designed for trail running offers greater flexibility, which is needed when running on a less stable surface. The tradeoff is that you lose some of the support of your normal training shoes.

RUNNING ACCESSORIES

Pulse/Heart Monitors

These devices, which monitor your heart rate while running, are gaining a large following, especially among serious runners. Why have they become so popular in the running world? The single biggest reason is that they can help you run more efficiently. Having a constant gauge of your heart rate available during your runs helps to ensure that the easy days stay easy and the hard ones remain solid.

Upon first using a heart monitor, many runners realize that they have been going too fast on their easy days. The experts recommend training at 70 percent of your maximum heart rate during your easy runs. On harder days, shoot for 80-85 percent of your maximum heart rate. You can use the reading during the end of your next road race as a measure of your maximum heart rate. Wearing the monitor while racing can also help you avoid the mistake of going out too fast at the start.

Less serious runners can use a heart monitor to measure how much fat they are burning during a workout. Many runners strap it on when they are engaging in other sports such as biking or the use of a fitness machine. Most models are capable of charting your heart rate over a period of time, and can be programmed to beep if you go above or below a preset level. They range in price from $150 to $250.

Water Bottle Belts

A water bottle attached to a belt that can be strapped around your waist is a good way to quench your thirst during those summer runs. It's lightweight and easy to drink from while running, though some runners still find the belt to be a bit cumbersome. In really hot weather, you might want to consider freezing the water before heading out. A water bottle and belt usually range in price from $15 to $20.

Running Watches

A running watch is an essential accessory for all levels of runners. It's more important to gauge your performance based on time rather than distance, especially for beginners. It's also much easier. Intermediate and advanced runners are more apt to take advantage of the various features running watches provide. An example is the countdown mode, which can be set to beep for a specified amount of time. This is great for surge running or interval workouts off of a track. The lap button feature offers you a breakdown of your mile times or other splits during a race or long run. Make sure the watch has memory storage and a light for night running. You don't have to pay a lot of money for a good watch. A watch including all these features can be bought for $40 or less.

Running Socks

Having trouble with blisters? If you are, it's worth buying socks designed especially for runners. Studies have shown that socks composed of all cotton or a mixture of cotton and synthetic fibers cause more blistering than socks consisting of 100 percent synthetic materials such as acrylics or nylon blends. The synthetic socks are better at keeping the perspiration away from the skin. I was surprised to find out that thicker socks usually cause less blistering than thin socks. Running socks can be purchased for around $6.00 a pair.

RUNNING ACCESSORIES YOU DON'T NEED

These days you can receive a running catalog in the mail that's almost the size of your local telephone book. Many of the items offered are worth buying, but some are not. Unless your eyes are highly sensitive to the sun, you probably don't need a pair of running sunglasses. They're expensive, usually costing $100 or more, and frequently cause you to perspire more. A better option for protecting yourself from the sun is wearing a cap with a long bill.

The popularity of sports drinks has remained high thanks to expensive marketing campaigns. Personally, I've almost become addicted to Gatorade. But, the truth is, water works just as well, if not better, than the various fancy fluid replacement drinks. In fact, many of the sport drinks contain too much sugar. Save yourself some money and stick to water.

Finally, as I discussed in the running shoes section, avoid buying top priced running shoes. You don't need to spend $100 or more to find a shoe that caters to your special needs. The best buys are in the $65-$85 range. Spend the difference on a good pasta dinner!

4. THE NOVICE RUNNER

You may be wondering how a former college cross country captain, a 2:38 marathoner and a self-described compulsive racer can understand the challenge facing a novice runner with little or no training. Anticipating this dilemma, I took it upon myself to become thoroughly out of shape for extended periods of time before starting to run again. This was no easy task. For periods that lasted months (and in more than one instance years) I forced myself to indulge in a daily routine that rivaled some of the most dedicated couch potatoes, marginal weekend warriors, and all-night partygoers.

I began to associate with a wide array of non-runners. I learned the best cure for a five margarita night was lots of sleep, followed by a long leisurely brunch, and then a nap in preparation for the next night's activities. Making the effort to eat sensibly no longer made sense.

With all this "base training" under my belt, I decided to lace up an old pair of running shoes and hit the road again. I was no longer motivated enough to go it alone, so I joined up with a couple of friends from work. I exposed my body and mind to the struggles of the recreational runner. I learned plenty.

WHY RUN?
Most of us in this health-conscious age are well aware of all the physical benefits offered by running. Besides producing leaner bodies, running has been found to reduce the risk of heart disease, high blood pressure and diabetes. Running helps to increase the

proportion of beneficial HDL cholesterol and lower the level of harmful LDL cholesterol. It also increases the body's maximum oxygen uptake up to 40 percent, improving circulation and pulmonary functions.

If all these medically proven health benefits are not enough to motivate you, try the rationale used by my friend, Chuck. He runs for desserts. Chuck loves cheese cake, chocolate cake, apple pie with ice cream and French pastries just to name a few. But he feels guilty about constantly indulging in these treats unless he gets in four to five runs a week. Chuck's commitment to running provides him with a clear conscience, along with a stable weight.

Speaking of weight, here's a statistic worthy of concern. A recent Harris poll found that 71 percent of adult Americans are overweight. Of those surveyed, 22 percent exceed their recommended weight by more than 20 percent. For years, doctors and national health associations have recommended 30 minutes a day of light to moderate exercise, but recent studies indicate that only 22 percent of us are meeting that standard. Finally, a Center for Disease Control study revealed that 24 percent of Americans fall into the "Rush Limbaugh" category – they are completely sedentary.

Running is more than just a means for combating these alarming physical fitness trends. It also provides numerous mental benefits. Personally, running has taught me how to keep my composure when faced with the many pressures of daily life. It serves as a healthy outlet for letting off steam during times of stress. The sport offers a terrific venue in which to calmly analyze whatever problem is most pressing. Or, if you are not in the mood to confront what's bothering you at the moment, running can serve as a temporary escape or respite from your troubles.

THINGS TO CONSIDER BEFORE HEADING OUT

One of the major reasons so many people are attracted to the sport of running is its uncomplicated nature. You don't have to take lessons, travel long distances, wait in lines or spend a significant amount of money for equipment to get started. For most newcomers, the preparation stage involves a trip to a sporting goods store for a pair of running shoes and a basic understanding of how running is going to affect your body. Taking the time to engage in a few precautionary practices is certain to enhance your experience. That's a good thing. With running, like so much else in life, first impressions will go a long way in determining your basic feelings about running. The more positive your initial reaction, the more likely you'll stick with it.

Running Shoes

Let's start with running shoes. (For a more detailed rundown, refer to the running shoes section in the Weather and Running Attire chapter.) Don't make the mistake of starting your new running adventure in a pair of tennis, basketball or even cross-training shoes. There's a good reason why there are shoes made specifically for running; there are many variables specific to the sport that are taken into consideration such as balance, cushioning, stability and inner-arch support. As someone new to running, with a body unaccustomed to the demands of the sport, you need the advantages of these shoes even more than an accomplished runner.

If you happen to have an old worn out pair of running shoes in your closet, leave them there. Running in worn out sneakers is one of the leading causes of injury in the sport. The risk is even higher if you've been using the shoes for activities other than running.

Try to purchase your shoes at a running specialty store. The salespeople at a running store can usually do a better job of helping you find the shoe that's right for you. You don't need to spend $100 to ensure that you're running in a quality shoe. Most of the top brand running shoe manufacturers such as Nike, Asics, Saucony and others have models in the $55-$85 range that match the needs of most runners and especially those of beginners.

Stretching

I recommend stretching as part of your routine running plan. Ideally, it would be best to stretch before starting, after warming up and after completing your run. But since we don't live in a perfect world, I don't expect you to always do all three. Try to at least remain committed to stretching both before and after a run.

Many beginners are unaware of the importance of stretching after they run. We all had to stretch before gym class, but never after. Stretching after a run gives you the opportunity to work out some of the kinks at a time when your muscles and tendons are warm and loose. Studies have shown that warm tissue muscle stretches better than cold tissue. This helps to reduce the risk of injury.

There is also tangible benefit to devoting as little as 5-10 minutes after your run to stretching. Your legs are apt to feel less like a couple of giant tree trunks at the start of your next run. The more stretching you do after a run, the more relaxed your muscles will feel at the beginning of the next run. Don't use stretching after a run as an excuse for not doing it before. I have to admit at times I have been guilty of blowing off the pre-run stretch, especially on cold days. What's the point of stretching muscles that are cold and tight? It's always better to stretch cold and tight muscles before a run than to not stretch at all. Even loosening them up a small amount can mean the difference between suffering an injury down the road or avoiding it.

The three most important legs muscles to stretch are the calf, the quadriceps and the hamstring. For recommendations on specific stretches for these muscle areas and others, refer to the stretching section of the *Injuries and How to Avoid Them* chapter.

Running in Hot & Cold Weather

When you're at the running store picking up your new shoes, don't feel obligated to buy all the various running accessories, such as the $170 Gortex running outfit. While it's important to protect yourself against mother nature's harsher days – hot, cold, wet – it's easy to go overboard and purchase a lot of unnecessary and expensive gear.

Hot weather poses the gravest danger to runners, especially inexperienced ones. The best defense against the heat is drinking plenty of water before heading out. Avoid gulping down glasses of water within a half hour or so before the run. It's tough enough dealing with the heat, the last thing you want to do is add a cramp to your troubles. You may want to consider taking along a water bottle on hot days. Many running stores sell water bottles that attach to lightweight belts. It's o.k. to stop and drink constantly during the run, but limit each break to one cup or less of water.

The risks of suffering heat exhaustion and becoming dehydrated rise significantly in hot and humid weather, especially for runners unaccustomed to these conditions. Once the mercury rises above 80 degrees and the humidity exceeds 50 percent, be careful. Always err on the side of caution. For beginners, it makes a whole lot more sense to opt for air conditioning or the pool, rather than playing the hero and trying to battle extremely hot weather.

Cold weather is generally easier to deal with. The good news about cold weather (except in the case of extreme conditions) is that you can always compensate for the temperature by dressing up. (Unfortunately, on hot days, the law of diminishing returns pretty much peaks once you're down to a tee-shirt and shorts.) The best defense against the cold and wind is to head out in thin layers of clothing. It will keep you warmer, as well as offer you more freedom of movement during your run than loose and heavy sweats. The inner layers of clothing should be the thinnest and the tightest. Sweatpants and tops composed primarily of nylon usually make good outer layers, especially on windy days.

Many novice runners make the mistake of wearing too much below their waist and not enough above it when running in cold weather with the theory being that since the legs are used the most, they need more protection against the cold. Actually, the parts of your body that you use the least need the most protection since these areas don't get as warmed up as your legs. Before I consider wearing more than one layer on my legs the temperature must drop below the 20-25 degree range. Two important areas to always remember to keep covered once the temperature starts dipping below the 40 degrees mark are your hands and ears.

Generally, beginners need to compensate a bit more for the cold weather than more experienced runners. It's more difficult to keep your body warm running at a slower pace. Let me offer an example of what you might want to wear on a typical 35 degree winter day.

Without getting bogged down on the advantages of the latest high-tech materials with names like polypropylene (see the *Weather and Running Attire* chapter) I suggest the following: for your legs – a pair of nylon sweatpants, on top – a thin short-sleeve T-shirt, followed by either a thicker long-sleeve tee-shirt or a thin sweatshirt, topped off with lightweight nylon jacket, and finally a cheap pair of gardening gloves and either a wool hat or a winter headband that covers your ears. For additional information on how to deal with hot and cold weather refer to the *Weather and Running Attire* chapter.

Finally, give yourself three to four hours to digest a major meal before running. Put off the unhealthy snacks – potato chips, diet sodas, etc. – until after the run. Once you're within an hour of your run, try to cut off even the healthy snacks such as fruit and granola bars. Believe me, your stomach and intestines will thank you.

TRAINING GUIDE FOR BEGINNERS
Level 1: For those Really Out of Shape Types
People who fall into this category engage in minimal or no aerobic type exercise. They might occasionally get on a bike or play tennis on the weekend, but not on a routine basis. They typically have no running experience. In the past, they never felt the need to be fitness oriented. Now, however, as they grow older, they're beginning to worry about their weight, or their overall health. They turn to running in the hope of limiting some of the collateral damage to both the mind and body brought on by the aging process.

The good news for those who fall into this category is my suggested training programs give you plenty of time to ease into the process. The first thing you have to do is to get into the habit of setting aside about an hour three days a week. Don't worry, you will not be running for the entire hour. You need time to get ready, stretch before and after the run, and recover. Try to set aside an hour on two weekdays and one weekend day.

I suggest you start out with a combination of brisk walking and jogging. For the first two weeks, try alternating two minutes of walking with two minutes of jogging for a total of 20-25 minutes.

As you get further along in the walk-jog, be conscious of maintaining the specified intervals of walking and jogging. Try not to be tempted into doing too much too soon if this seems easy at first. Why ruin a good buzz with a hangover the next day? You have plenty of time to improve.

Over the next two weeks, work towards increasing the total time of the "run" to 30 minutes. Start increasing the ratio of the time jogging to walking. For example, in the third week, start with two minutes of walking followed by three minutes of jogging for a total of 25 minutes. By the fourth week, make the minor adjustment of working out every other day instead of just three specific days a week.

At the end of four weeks your "run" should be up to 30 minutes, with most of the time spent jogging not walking. Aim to get your jogging to walking ratio up to three to one. While I'm hitting you with a variety of ratios and times to keep track of, one thing you don't need to preoccupy yourself with is the speed of your jogging. Jog at whatever pace feels comfortable. It's far more important to keep the jogging phase consistent than to have momentary bursts of speed that leave you ending up at a pace no faster than walking.

Now you're ready for the big time: a series of uninterrupted runs. Starting in the fifth week or so, begin jogging without any walking breaks for 20 minutes. Use the first five minutes as a warmup by starting out at a somewhat slower pace than may feel natural. Try to maintain a consistent pace throughout the rest of the run, but don't get discouraged if you begin to tire and slow down a bit towards the end.

There are always going to be days when you're not going to feel that great, and most, if not all, of the run is a struggle. Try to remember during those early, trying times that the more often you're able to get through those days, the less often they will occur in the future. Also, keep in mind that you're going to feel the worst at the beginning of a run. Your legs are tight and your breathing might start out a bit abnormal, causing you to cramp up a bit. You have to stick with it and wait it out. Remind yourself that you are going to feel better once you get further into the run.

Limit the run to 20-22 minutes for two weeks. At the beginning of the next week (week 7 overall), increase the time of the run to 25 minutes. Your goal by the end of the eighth week is to be able to jog for 25 minutes at a comfortable pace. Congratulations are in order once you make it to this stage. You've crossed the most difficult threshold of running, which is getting in shape enough to actually enjoy the sport. Go out and celebrate with all your non-running, still out of shape, friends.

LEVEL 1 TRAINING SCHEDULE

Weeks 1-2	*3 workouts, 20-25 minutes, 2:2 run/walk ratio*
Week 3	*3 workouts, 25-30 minutes, 3:2 run/walk ratio*
Week 4	*every other day, 30 minutes, 3:1 run/walk ratio*
Weeks 5-6	*every other day, 20 minutes, all running*
Weeks 7-8	*every other day, 25 minutes, all running*

Level 2: Somewhat Active Types

These are the health club enthusiasts, weekend warriors, former college jocks, and people addicted to perfecting one sport other than running. Their running experience, if any, usually dates back to a long time ago. Their reasons for taking up running vary. Some have friends who run and want to join in on the fun. For others, a hectic work schedule might preclude them from taking part in their favorite athletic activity. Some may be concerned about gaining weight. Whatever their reasons, they all see running as a new means for satisfying the fitness bug craving within them.

If you fall into this category, the transition to running will not be too difficult if you keep your expectations in check during the early stages.

Don't expect to master the sport of running at the level you're accustomed to performing more familiar athletic activities. I know it looks easy enough and a "one foot in front of the other" mindset may sct in before you start. But keep in mind that running uses your muscles and offers a cardiovascular workout that varies significantly from most other popular sports. Also, remember that the beginning of the run is always the worst. As you get further into a run and warm up, your body relaxes, making it easier to enjoy the run.

Start out running every other day for the first couple of weeks. Don't worry about the pace of your runs. Take the beginning of each run slow. After a few minutes, work up to a pace you feel comfortable with maintaining for the rest of the run. I recommend beginning with a run of 20-25 minutes. This doesn't sound like much of a workout, but it will serve as a good base to build on.

Beginning in the third week and continuing into the fourth week, consider running two days in a row, taking a day off after the two runs. Try increasing the first of the two runs to around 30 minutes, while keeping the second run equal to the 20-25 minute time period you were doing for the first two weeks. Targeting the first day for the long run allows you to use the second day to work out the kinks in your legs muscles before taking a day of rest. If you do the longer run on the second day, the chances are greater that your legs will feel tighter on the run after the day off.

Over the next two weeks (weeks five and six), try to accomplish two things. First, increase the number of runs in a row to three. Second, attempt to raise all your runs to the 30 minute level. Use the first week to get comfortable with running three days in a row. During the second week, concentrate on reaching the 30 minute mark. The runs don't have to all be exactly 30 minutes, but try not to let them vary by more than a half a mile or five minutes.

LEVEL 2 TRAINING SCHEDULE

Weeks 1-2	*every other day, 20-25 minutes*
Weeks 3-4	*2 runs in a row, 1st 30 minutes,*
	2nd 20-25 minutes
Weeks 5-6	*3 runs in a row, 30 minutes each.*

By the end of six weeks, you should be feeling fairly comfortable with your new running routine. Those "down" days when most of the body and especially your legs feel tired or tight will happen less frequently. Plus, without having to make any extra effort, the pace you feel comfortable running at will begin to gradually increase. Keep this all up and you'll be in the best shape of your life.

TAKING THE NEXT STRIDE: STICKING TO A PLAN

It's no easy task to stick to a running schedule over the long haul. There are plenty of situations that can distract you from staying on course. A busy work schedule, vacations, a desire to play other sports, minor illnesses, injuries, adverse weather and a general lack of motivation are common hurdles. You have a measure of control over some of these, others you do not. The trick is to keep as many of these variables in check, without letting the ones that you have no control over get the best of you.

There's not much you can do about a touch of the flu or a nasty cold, except to wait it out. In fact, trying to run when you still feel weak is only going to extend the amount of time you're out of action. Similarly, if you're forced to work long hours for a period of time, running may have to take a back seat to your professional pursuits. This makes it even more important that you don't let some of the other possibilities, such as a lack of motivation or a light rain, put you off track from your running routine.

Back to Level 1 Beginners

At this point, you have mastered jogging for 25 minutes every other day. Concentrate on being able to maintain this running schedule over the long-term. I recommend waiting at least a couple of months before considering increasing the distance or frequency of your runs. From a fitness standpoint, consistency is the key objective.

Don't make the mistake of remaining dedicated to your running routine at any cost. There's a fine line between staying committed and losing your common sense. Don't hesitate to take some time off if slight soreness in your knee turns into a constant feeling of pain (turn to the *Injuries and How to Avoid Them* chapter for more information) or a bad cold has you feeling rundown. When you do return, don't make the mistake of overcompensating for the lost time. In fact, if you're coming back after taking off more than a week, resume by doing a bit less than your average workout. For example, limit your runs to 20 minutes for the first week back. What you don't want to do is to start running two days in a row in order to make up for lost time.

If after a period of time you feel the urge to raise your amount of running, do it gradually. One possibility is to start running two days in a row. Keep the distance of the runs equal to your current rate. You don't want to be increasing two variables – distance and frequency – at the same time. Take a couple of weeks to make the transition to the two days on, one day off schedule.

In a few weeks, increase the distance of your runs. Again, do it gradually. Add just a few minutes to your run. For example, if you had been running about 25 minutes, spend a few weeks raising it to 30 minutes. Go from 25 to 28 the first two weeks, and then raise it to an even 30 minutes in the third week.

Let's review how long it might take to get to this point. First, take two months just getting use to your new running routine discussed in the first section. Next, take two weeks becoming accustomed to running two days in a row. Keep this new schedule up for one month. Three and a half months later, start increasing the distance of your runs. After more than four months have passed, you may find it comfortable doing two 30 minute runs in two consecutive days. However, this is all optional. You don't have to go beyond maintaining the level achieved after the first eight weeks.

Back to Level 2 Beginners

You're gotten to a point of running three days in a row for about 30 minutes per run. Where do you go from here? You have several options. First, you can stay where you're at. As I suggested to level 1 beginners, there's nothing wrong with just maintaining your current level of training for the long-term. The fitness gains are significant, while the risk of injury remains low. You're already ahead of the game.

For some of you, this isn't going to be enough. The old competitive spirit in you wants to take another step up the running ladder. If you fall into this category, keep in mind that raising your level of training is going to put more stress on your body than increasing the resistance a notch or two on a stationary bike or stairmaster. One of the golden rules of running is never increase your mileage by more than 10 percent a week. For a beginner, I recommend extending the time frame to a few weeks.

For example, consider running four days in a row instead of three, keeping the distance of the run equal to what you have been doing. Give yourself a few weeks to get accustomed to the extra day of running without a break. Once you're comfortable with this new routine, try lengthening two of your four runs by about a half-mile the first week. That's equivalent to four to five minutes. Over the next two weeks, up the distance by about a mile (eight to ten minutes) over the original distance.

I recommend that you target the first and third runs for the longer outings. As I mentioned in the first section, it's not a good idea to take a day off after the longest run in your regular routine. Think of the fourth day as the equivalent of getting a massage before going to bed after a long day of hiking. If you just go to bed after the hike, you're far more likely to wake up the next day feeling tight than if you had gotten the massage. Similarly, your first day back is likely to feel better if you end your four days in a row with one of the easier runs.

Let's review what you have accomplished. In about six weeks, you're up to running four days in a row. The first and third run have increased to approximately 40 minutes, while the other two remain at 30 minutes. Keep this up and you're certain to shed your beginner status. In fact, you might want to consider running a 10-K sometime in the future. Take a peek at the 10-K training chapter!

5. 10-K TRAINING

One of the most enjoyable aspects of running is participating in **10-K races**. Running a 10-K on a Saturday or Sunday morning is a great way to begin a weekend day.

The rise in popularity of 10-K road races has broadened their appeal to runners of all ages and levels of ability. They offer the competitive entrants the opportunity to test their running skills against fellow runners, or against their past performances. Picking off a couple of local rivals and running a good time always makes my weekend.

For the less competitive, the races are, to put it simply, just plain fun. You get great companionship during the run, a t-shirt to show for your efforts, and usually some good eats and conversation after the race. Some races even have beer!

One of the best parts of 10-Ks is that you don't have to drastically modify your normal training habits in order to run them. Unlike the marathon, which involves months of intensive training targeted towards a single race, only minor adjustments to your usual training schedule are required to accommodate running a number of 10-Ks in just one season.

The return from doing a marathon is similar to two bond traders flipping a coin on Friday for their pay checks. One could be in line for a big pay off or be left out in the cold. Running 10-Ks, however, promises more of a steady return for your efforts.

RUNNING FOR FUN: SUGGESTED TRAINING

Many runners choose to run 10-Ks just for the fun of it. Most don't care how fast they are going. Therefore, they are not preoccupied with finishing the race under a certain time. The 10-K distance – 6.2 miles – is probably longer than what they typically run on any given day. They usually run about every other day and cover 3-4 miles per run. They consider running a 10-K to be a good challenge, but don't feel obligated to prepare too seriously for it.

There are a few minor modifications to your usual routine you may want to consider if you fall into this category:

First, it's worth running for a short period on the day preceding the race. Running the day before helps to keep your legs feeling loose during the race. You don't have to go far. Run until your legs feel warmed up enough to get a good stretch in afterwards. This will ensure that your leg muscles are loose from the start. This is important because participating in a race with many other runners will probably cause you to start out a bit faster than your usual training pace.

Second, it's a good idea to go for a run on the day following the race. You will end up running three days in a row, but it's worth it. Running the day after helps to work out all the kinks in your legs that are likely to result from running further and a bit harder than your usual day of training. Again, you don't have to run too far. A couple of miles followed by a good stretch will do the trick. This will get you back to normal in time for your next run. Without the short run the day after, you're likely to feel pretty lousy on that next outing.

Third, every 10 to 14 days run further than your usual distance. You don't want the experience of running a 10-K to be a complete mystery. Psychologically as well as physically, you will benefit from running 6-7 miles at least once every time prior to doing a 10-K.

Going into the race knowing that you can go the distance builds confidence. It makes the last couple of miles easier to complete.

TIPS FOR RACE DAY

Get yourself out of bed early on race day. Ideally, if you are going to eat something before the race, you want to get it down two hours or more before race time. I recommend eating something light and easy to digest. A bagel, light on the cream cheese, or a few pancakes, light on the butter, are both fine. A couple of eggs and strips of bacon are not. Try to stick to water over milk or orange juice before the race. Dairy products and citric juices have a habit of playing tricks with your stomach while you are running when ingested too close to race time.

A good rule to always follow when it comes to food: *spoil yourself after the race, not before.*

Try to show up at the race site a half-hour or more prior to the start of the run. This allows you time to warm up a bit before the gun goes off. It's always a good idea to get in a brief easy jog and good stretch before the race. The whole process only takes 15 to 20 minutes to complete. I recommend an easy jog of about five minutes followed by ten minutes of basic stretching exercises.

You might wonder why you should bother to take the time to warm up for a 10-K. It's important because you are likely to run the race both harder and longer than your routine run. Even though you don't intend to take the 10-K too seriously, you're still bound to exert yourself more than usual. The crowd of people participating and watching will inspire you to push yourself more than you might have anticipated going into the race. You need your legs loose and ready for the extra effort.

Try not to make the mistake of starting out too fast once the gun goes off. Many novice runners have the habit of getting too excited by the crowds. They feel inclined to shoot for a moment of glory near the front of the pack at the start of the race. Stay calm and save your sprint for the 100 yards before the finish line. A quick start is likely to come back to haunt you soon after. It also creates a minor inconvenience for more advanced runners who have to swerve around those who suddenly slow down.

On a hot day, consider stopping for one or two water breaks during the race. Once the temperature rises above 70 degrees in humid weather, you have to begin worrying about keeping yourself properly hydrated. While stopping for water can be regarded as an option when the temperature is in the 70s, I consider it a necessity once the mercury goes above the low 80s, especially if you don't have much experience with running in the heat.

Most 10-K races have a few water stations on the course where you can grab a cup of water. A few runners have mastered the technique of being able to pick up a cup of water and drink it almost without breaking stride. It's a great trick, but not easy to do. For most of us, attempting to run while grabbing and drinking a cup of water leads to a lot of spilling and very little refreshment. I recommend slowing down to a walk while picking up the cup and drinking it. Certainly, if you are not worried about your time, you should be willing to take 10 seconds out of the race to stop for water.

Sticking with other runners of similar ability during a 10-K helps you maintain a consistent pace throughout the run. It's a whole lot easier to keep up the pace you ran for the first mile during the sixth if you have another runner or two to share the burden with you. Try to be conscious of who is around you after about two miles. Attempt to stay with that group of runners for the rest of the race.

Remember the concept that being able to play with other kids as a child was a sure sign of emotional development and mental potential? Running takes it one step further. Being able to run with others will ensure that your endurance remains high.

RUNNING FOR TIME: INTERMEDIATE LEVEL

Many runners participate in 10-Ks for the thrill of competition. They enjoy racing against others or just competing against themselves.

Let's call these fairly serious runners **intermediate runners**. Running for them is more than just an exercise they have chosen in order to stay in shape. They run as much for the mental satisfaction it brings to their lives as they do for the physical benefits. They run five to seven days a week and have been doing it for years. They may not be the fastest runner on the block, but they are among the most consistent. Running a 10-K offers them the opportunity to evaluate their training efforts on a quantitative basis.

Building a Base

If you fall into this category, the first thing you'll need to do is **build up a mileage base** during the off seasons. You will find that most of the popular 10-K races worth running are during the spring and the fall. Therefore, the winter and summer are good times for getting in a few months of uninterrupted, solid training.

During the 10-K season, your training will be determined to some extent by the races themselves. You'll have to allow for two easy runs on the days prior to and after the race, as well as devoting one day a week to concentrating on pace. The focus is on quality over quantity. Along with the higher intensity, there's also a higher risk of soreness or injury, which clearly can set back your training for a while.

In the off-season, however, there's little to distract you from sticking to a consistent running schedule. I recommend giving yourself a brief resting period between finishing up a season of 10-K running and beginning your base training.

Let's say you run your last 10-K of the year around Thanksgiving. Take it easy during the month of December. Devote your energies to celebrating the holidays with extra gusto. I'm not suggesting that you completely stop running. There's no reason to let yourself lose all that you have gained over the past fall. Just cut it back a bit. I suggest going out only three to four days a week and shortening the distance of the runs.

Once you have recovered from your New Year's celebration, it's time to get back to business. You will be well rested, but still in pretty good shape – the perfect combination for beginning your base training period. The requirements for establishing a base probably don't vary much from your usual workout routine. It's just that now you are using this training as a means to achieve a more important end result – running a better 10-K time. It's the foundation on which you will build. By the end of March, you will be ready to enter a training phase specifically targeted to racing at your highest potential over the next few months of 10-K running.

Try to run six days a week during the base training period. As I pointed out in the first chapter, your training schedule should be flexible enough to accommodate any unexpected problems with your body.

I can't stress this enough: never ignore a warning signal that your body is sending you. Don't rigidly stick to the training schedule at all costs.

THINK OF BASE TRAINING AS A BONUS

Consider this base training phase as an extra bonus round of training prior to the 10-K season. Realistically, you would probably still do pretty well without it. So don't let it destroy your upcoming spring running by letting it put you out of action. What's the point of putting more effort into your off-season training if it makes you unhealthy in the spring? In other words, don't overdo it!

Alternate between easier shorter runs and more solid longer runs over the six days of running per week. For instance, go a solid five to seven miles on Monday, Wednesday and Friday, and do an easy four on Tuesday, Thursday and Saturday, with Sunday as your off day. Or if you enjoy getting in a good run on the weekend, push the entire schedule up one day so that Monday becomes your off day.

Don't make the mistake of running long and hard the day before an off day. Many runners follow misguided reasoning in assuming that they might as well give it their all on the day preceding a rest day. Their attitude is: "I might as well double the workout since I'll be receiving double the rest afterwards." This reasoning is flawed. The day after a hard run should be used as a **recovery day**, not an off day.

Recovery days are just as important as the longer runs. They offer you the opportunity to loosen up and work out all the kinks and soreness that develop in your leg muscles from the more strenuous workouts. All of that tightness at the beginning of the run following a hard day becomes more difficult to loosen up and work out of your legs the longer you stay inactive. The sequence should be: *solid run – easy run – day off – solid run.*

Consider lengthening one or two of the longer runs of the week to the 7-8 mile range during the second month of base training. Your weekly mileage will begin to rise from 30 miles a week to around 33, with the goal of reaching 35 miles a week by the third month of base training. Extending the long runs will get you ready for the longer runs you will start doing periodically during training in the 10-K season.

Keep in the mind that all the distances recommended in this book are only offered as suggestions. Don't hesitate to adjust recommended mileage levels to cater to your individual needs. Two runners capable of running the same 10-K time frequently train at different mileage levels. Seven miles may be as far as one runner needs to go on a long day, whereas another runner may feel inclined to do 10 miles.

TABLE 1: TYPICAL OFF-SEASON BASE TRAINING WEEK, IN MILES

	M	**T**	**W**	**Th**	**F**	**S**	**Su**
Month 1	5-7	4	5-7	4	5-7	4	off
Month 2	5-7	4	7-8	4	5-7	4	off
Month 3	5-7	4	7-8	4	7-9	4	off

In-Season Training

The coming of spring and fall means it's time to show off your talents by entering a number of 10-Ks. Begin your in-season training by choosing the races you plan to enter well ahead of time. Try to achieve an adequate **balance** between committing time to training and racing. Keep in mind that every race costs you two to three days of training — the warm-up day before and the one to two days of recovery after. Limit yourself to one or two 10-Ks a month during the first two months of the season. This way you can still devote a good portion of your time to building up your endurance. Only during the final month should you attempt to race more than every other weekend.

I realize that it seems somewhat illogical to recommend racing less in order to work yourself into better shape. What could be a better workout than a tough race? Racing will help to make you a stronger runner. It's obviously an important component of your in-season training schedule. But it's not the only vital element for running faster times.

You must do more than just run a slew of races after getting in a solid off-season of training if your goal is to run the fastest possible time. You still have to get in a series of quality training runs in order to reduce your racing times further along in the season. You don't want to achieve your best race time only a month into the season, and then struggle for the rest of the spring just to match it. It's far more rewarding to continue to improve throughout the season and peak at the end.

It's unlikely that you will continue to improve if you simply race on the weekend and recover during the week. It may work in April, but it's going to cost you in May and June. Don't get upset if a few of your running buddies get the best of you early on. Right around the time they start to get overconfident, you will surge past them midway through the race and never look back.

There are two other important aspects to your in-season training besides racing. One is **surge** or **speed training**. The other is the **long run**. Both must be incorporated into your weekly training schedule for most of the 10-K season; both are covered below.

Speed Training

It's important that your legs are given one day a week to run a bit harder than your usual steady training pace. It keeps you from becoming permanently locked into one pace of running, and thereby limiting the potential for your leg muscles to supply greater leg speed. Greater leg speed allows you to cover more territory without exerting more energy. This leads to faster times.

There are two basic ways you can work on improving your speed. One method is to do **interval training** on a track. Locating a track to work out on is not difficult. Almost all high schools, colleges, and universities have tracks that are open to public use during evenings and weekends. Speed workouts on a track represent more of a radical departure from your usual training than the other option — the surge or quick-tempo run.

Generally, I only recommend speed workouts on a track for more advanced runners, or intermediate runners who are able to do the workout with others. Interval training is not easy. It can take a lot out of you, both mentally and physically. It helps some runners but discourages others.

Increasing Speed Through Surge Workouts

A **quick-tempo** or **surge run** is a more comfortable way to make the transition to speed for those lacking experience on a track. The idea behind the quick-tempo run is to choose distinct intervals during a run to surge for a limited time period. By surge, I mean to pick up speed, but not to the point of sprinting. The intent is to run harder than a pace you feel comfortable with, but not so hard that you feel winded at the end of the interval. In runner-speak, this sort of run is commonly referred to as a *fartlek* run. (The name was coined by runners in Sweden.)

After completing the surge or *fartlek*, it's important not to slow down beyond the comfortable pace you were maintaining before the surge. It defeats a major aspect of the run if you slow down below your normal pace between surges. Besides working on your leg speed, these runs build up your cardiovascular capacity by adjusting your breathing to the increase in your heart rate that results from the surge. If you slow down too much, you are letting your heart off the hook.

Use the first mile as a warm-up during a quick-tempo run. The pace should be relaxed and easy. Once you are about a mile into the run, begin doing surges for 90 seconds every three minutes. Run hard for 90 seconds, maintain your normal training pace for three minutes, and then do another 90 second surge. Repeat the process until you have done five 90 second surges. Finish up the run with an easy two mile warm-down.

TABLE 2: SUGGESTED WEEKLY SURGE WORKOUT	
Week 1	four 90 second surges every 3 minutes
Week 2	five 90 second surges every 3 minutes
Week 3	five 90 second surges every 3 minutes
Week 4	five 2 minute surges every 4 minutes
Week 5	six 2 minute surges every 4 minutes
Week 6	six 2 minute surges every 4 minutes
Week 7	six 90 second surges every 3 minutes
Week 8	six 2 minute surges every 4 minutes
Week 9	six 90 second surges every 3 minutes
Week 10	four 2 minute surges every 4 minutes
Week 11	four 90 second surges every 3 minutes
Week 12	no workout

Stick to this workout for the first few weeks. It will take a bit of time to adjust to these quick-tempo runs if you have never done them before. After about three weeks, try increasing the amount and duration of the surges. For instance, surge for two minutes every four minutes, and raise the total number of surges to six. As in the first few weeks, continue to start the run with an easy mile warm-up, and finish with a two mile warm-down.

After a couple of weeks of doing the longer version of the quick tempo run, I suggest alternating week to week between the two workouts for the next month. This will take you into the third and final month of your 10-K season. This is when you should run your best times. To keep your legs feeling fresh for the races climaxing your season, phase out the quick-tempo run from your weekly schedule during the third month.

For those of you adventurous enough to hit a track for your speed workouts, please refer to the recommendations found in Chapter 7, *Speed Training*.

The Long Run

The other key ingredient to your in-season training schedule is the **long run**. Add a run in the range of ten miles once a week in the beginning and the middle of the season. It can be a bit shorter or longer depending on your personal comfort level for long distance runs. Try to run at least eight miles, but don't go any further than eleven.

The long run serves two purposes. First, it helps to build up your **endurance and stamina**, the strength component of running. A "strong" runner does not falter during the second half of a race, or wilt in the heat. Second, the long runs offer you an important **mental advantage** on race days. It won't seem nearly as difficult to finish the 6.2 miles strong if you are consistently getting in runs four miles or longer.

Limit your long run to once every ten days to two weeks during the second half of racing season. In fact, you can completely eliminate the long run for the final two weeks.

Once you get within a couple of weeks of your final race of the season, don't overdo it. You don't have enough time to reap the benefits acquired from these endurance-building long runs. Many runners make the mistake of training too hard during the final weeks of racing. They fear that everything they have gained from months of training will be lost if they ease up a bit.

Actually, the opposite is true. If you don't begin to taper off your training in the end, you will not be able to race at your maximum potential. All those months of dedicated running allows you the luxury of easing up on your training so that your legs can be well-rested for your final races without suffering any endurance loss penalty.

Let's take a look at what a typical week would be like in the middle of your 10-K season. Let's say that you are planing to run a race on Saturday morning. The Monday preceding the race is a good day to get in your long run of ten miles. It's a good idea to put as much time as possible between your long run and the race during the week. You want to give your legs the maximum time to recover from your more intense training runs prior to racing.

The same holds true for your speed workout day. Try to give yourself at least a three day cushion between either the long run or speed workout and the 10-K. Therefore, Wednesday would be a good day for your quick-tempo run. Make Tuesday an easy run of three to four miles. It's important to allow yourself a day of recovery between the two toughest workouts of the week.

THE IMPORTANCE OF RECOVERY DAYS

Don't underestimate the value of taking it easy on your recovery days. These days enable you to remain fresh for your more intense runs of the week. Remember, it means a whole lot more to do your long and quick-tempo runs solidly on a consistent basis, than it is to add a couple of miles or quicken the pace of your easy run.

Target Thursday for a run of 4-5 miles. It's the one run of the week that will probably most resemble what your average day of running was like prior to following a training schedule. It's neither an easy or hard day. Friday, as you might expect, should be a light day of running, given that it's the day before the race. An easy 2-3 miles will do the trick. The point is to run long enough on Friday so that your leg muscles are loose and ready for a good stretch afterwards. Get in a run the day after racing. Don't take off the day after a race. Take your day off two days after running a 10-K.

TABLE 3: 12 WEEK IN-SEASON 10-K TRAINING SCHEDULE - INTERMEDIATE

	M	T	W	Th	F	S	Su
Week 1	8-10	3-4	6	srg	4-5	8	off
Week 2	8-11	3-4	srg	6	2-3	10K	3-6
Week 3	off	8-11	3-4	srg	4-5	8	6
Week 4	off	8-10	3-4	srg	4-5	8	off
Week 5	8-11	3-4	srg	4-5	2-3	10K	3-6
Week 6	off	8-10	3-4	srg	4-5	8	off
Week 7	8-11	3-4	srg	4-5	2-3	10K	3-6
Week 8	off	7-8	3-4	srg	4-5	8	off
Week 9	8-11	3-4	srg	4-5	2-3	10K	3-6
Week 10	off	8	3-4	srg	4-5	8	off
Week 11	7-8	3-4	srg	4-5	2-3	10K	3-6
Week 12	off	4	5-6	4	2-3	10K	3-6

Note: "srg" = surge

Running the day after the race is important. It gives you the opportunity to work out all the kinks that develop in your leg muscles as a result of the extra effort you put out running a race. Waiting an extra day will make it more difficult to loosen up those sore, tight muscles. Without the run the day after, you're likely to feel pretty lousy on your next run.

The post-race day run does not have to be that long. Let your condition determine the distance of the run. If your legs are still real tired, just go a few miles. If they don't feel that bad, shoot for five or six miles.

I'm still a believer in taking one day off a week. It's important to give both your body and mind a day of rest from running. The exception to this rule is for the weeks when you are racing. You still get a day off. But the "week" of training is stretched into eight days. In a week that you are not racing, you can incorporate the day off into the conventional seven day period.

RUNNING FOR TIME: ADVANCED LEVEL

There's a group of runners out there who place too much emphasis on running a fast 10-K time. I know, I used to be one. I'm now a recovering 10-K "runaholic." Not by choice, of course. I've just become a bit lazier over the past couple of years. Some of us ran competitively in college and still yearn for the thrill of racing. Others are more serious about running today than they were in their early years. They're always in good shape and look forward to every upcoming 10-K season as an opportunity to lower their previous best times. Typically, we are talking about men who are capable of running under 40 minutes and women who can cross the finish line under 45 minutes.

If you fall into this category, there's a few points you might want to consider incorporating into your training routine if you haven't already done so. First, unlike less advanced runners, you probably will not have to set aside time for developing a solid base. I'm not suggesting that advanced runners should eliminate base training as part of their 10-K training schedule. For the most part, your routine training should provide you with a sufficient base from which to begin in-season 10-K training.

The structure of your in-season training will resemble the format offered in the prior section for intermediate runners. Try to put together a schedule that lasts about 12 weeks. Run a race on average once every two weeks, but race more frequently towards the end of the 12 week season. The thrust behind your training is also similar. The two big days of the week are still the long run and the speed workout. You will raise the intensity level of these days up a notch by running a bit longer and faster. The **long runs** should be in the range of 11 to 12 miles. Scale it back to 8 to 10 miles during the final four weeks of racing. Towards the end of the season, put less emphasis on endurance-building runs and more on ensuring that your legs are well rested for the final races.

The **speed workouts** (also known as **interval training**) involve doing repeat intervals on a track. One of the reasons interval workouts on a track are necessary for the advanced runner is that they simulate racing conditions. They also serve to improve your leg muscle strength, running style, and mental toughness.

Interval training consists of running short distances ranging from 200 meters to a mile at a speed equal to or below your actual race pace. A complete speed workout includes a series of intervals with a brief rest period between each effort. Please refer to Chapter 7, *Speed Training*, for specific workout recommendations.

A Typical Race Week

Let's see what your typical week midway through the 10-K season would look like. We'll make this one of the weeks that you plan to run a 10-K on Saturday morning. Do your long run the **Monday** preceding the race. The same rule holds true for advanced runners as for the intermediate group – put as much time as possible between your long run and the race during the week.

For **Tuesday**, take an easy run in the range of five to six miles. Don't make the mistake of downplaying the significance of what I referred to earlier as the *recovery days*. These days allow you to recover from the more intense workouts of the week. You can designate **Wednesday** as your speed day on the track.

On **Thursday**, get in a run of six to seven miles. It's the one run of the week that will most resemble what your average day of running was like prior to following a training schedule. The pace should be steady, not too hard, not too easy. The day before racing, should be a light day of running. An easy three to four miles will do the trick on **Friday** — and try to get in a good stretch after Friday's run.

TABLE 4: 12 WEEK 10-K TRAINING SCHEDULE - ADVANCED RUNNERS

	M	T	W	Th	F	S	Su
Week 1	11-12	5-6	speed	6-7	10	7-8	off
Week 2	11-12	5-6	speed	6-7	3-4	10K	5-8
Week 3	off	11-12	5-6	speed	6-7	5-6	srg
Week 4	7-8	11-12	5-6	speed	6	srg	off
Week 5	11-12	5-6	speed	6-7	3-4	10K	5-8
Week 6	off	11-12	5-6	speed	6-7	srg	6
Week 7	11-12	5-6	speed	6-7	3-4	10K	5-8
Week 8	off	11-12	5-6	speed	6-7	srg	5-6
Week 9	10	4	speed	6	3-4	10K	5-8
Week 10	off	8-10	4	speed	6	7-8	off
Week 11	8-10	4	speed	6	3-4	10K	4-6
Week 12	off	4	speed	6	2-3	10K	4-6

It's always a good idea to run the day following a race. The length of the run can vary. If your post-race condition is not that bad, try shooting for seven to eight miles. If your leg muscles are feeling really tight, limit the run to four to five miles.

Take a day off in the week following a race only after you have given yourself an opportunity to work out all those post-race kinks in your legs. So essentially, your race day "week," when you include your day off, becomes an eight day week.

During the early and middle parts of the season in weeks you're not racing, add a quick-tempo run to your training routine. On page 52, I introduced the Swedish term *fartlek* to describe this sort of run. Unlike the intensity of intervals on a track, it lets you improve your speed and endurance capabilities more in line with your usual training habits. The idea behind the quick-tempo run is to choose distinct intervals during a run to surge for a limited time period. More details on structuring the run can be found in the section for intermediate runners, pages 47-57.

Don't get too concerned about running fast times early in the season. It's better to maintain a fairly demanding training schedule for the first half of the season, even if it means you run a couple of your first 10-Ks on tired legs. The payoff in lower than expected times during the last month of racing will make it all worth it.

Keeping up the mileage during the first half of your training season gives you the luxury of cutting back on the miles during the last four weeks. It lets you to go into your final races with rested legs, without reducing your well-earned high level of endurance.

---

5 THINGS TO REMEMBER: 10-K TRAINING
1. Build up a solid base during the off-season.
2. Set aside a specific period for in-season training:
   I recommend 12 weeks.
3. Add a speed or fartlek day to your training routine.
4. Set aside a day each week for a long run.
5. Emphasize quality over quantity at the end of the season.

RUNNING FOR TIME: TIPS FOR RACE DAY

It's a great feeling to be able to parlay months of serious training into a fast 10-K time. Running a new personal best time is the perfect reward for your efforts. It's also very satisfying to consistently finish ahead of your local rivals during the season. Racing effectively also builds your confidence in the ability to perform under pressure in other aspects of your life.

Also, unlike the marathon, where if you have a bad race you have to wait months or even a year to get another chance, you only have to wait for the next weekend to find another 10-K to erase the memories of a poor performance.

What to Eat

It's a good idea to wake up at least three hours before race time. Try to avoid eating anything within two hours of the race. Have a light breakfast. Stay away from meat and dairy products. Bacon and eggs and a glass of milk is definitely out. Don't drink orange juice or any other citrus drink. The acidic nature of these juices have a habit of playing tricks with your stomach if consumed before running. Stick to drinking water prior to racing.

Breakfast suggestions include: a bagel without cream cheese, a couple of fluffy pancakes light on the butter and syrup, or a banana and cereal with skim milk or water in place of regular milk. Eat a good dinner the night before so that you are not tempted to overeat in the morning prior to the race.

The Warm-Up

Arrive at the race site 45 minutes to an hour prior to the starting time. You want to make sure you have plenty of time to **warm-up** and stretch after waiting in line to pick up your racing number. Warm up with an easy five to ten minute jog — closer to five minutes on a warm day and ten minutes on a cold day.

The warm-up run is important for two reasons. First, you want to loosen up your legs enough to get in a good ten minutes of stretching prior to the start of the race. The second reason builds on the first. Your legs have to be ready from the start to run hard.

When you're racing for time, you don't have the luxury of using the first couple of miles to get yourself in gear to run faster.

Get Off to a Good Start

You want to get off to a good start once the gun goes off. Start fast, but don't get carried away. A strong start helps you avoid becoming stuck for a while with a mass of weaker runners. In every 10-K there is always a bunch of weekend warriors who start out running far beyond their abilities. Their goal is to obtain that one moment of glory before fading fast. A strong start lessens the likelihood of having to deal with these participants.

You also want to get off to a good start to position yourself early with the caliber of runners you hope to be able to stick with for the remainder of the race. If you're not with them early, it will be difficult if not impossible to catch up to them later. The group of runners you are matching strides with at a mile and half to two miles into the race are the ones you are most likely to finish with.

You do have to be careful about not going for broke early on. Don't let the excitement of the race cause you to start out too fast. Let's say your goal is to run a time that averages a six and a half minute-per-mile pace. It's okay to start out a bit under 6:30, say around 6:10-6:15, to get yourself in a good position. What you should not do is to go through the first mile at a clip under six minutes. If you do that, you'll start to fade before you even reach two miles. Your confidence, not to mention much of your body, will be shot for the rest of the race.

Set a Pace & Stay Consistent

The goal between **miles two and five** is to stay consistent. You have to push yourself to keep from falling off your per-mile-pace or slipping behind the pack running at your level. In other words, you have to work harder just to keep up with the pace. Let the other runners help you out. It's far easier to run with or immediately behind someone than it is to do it alone. Take turns sharing the responsibility of maintaining the pace.

After **four miles**, it's worth the risk of dipping under your planned per-mile-pace, if you're able, so that you don't lose contact with the pack you've been running with. In fact, being able to stay with these guys during the second half of the race is the key ingredient for improving the chances of setting a new personal best time. Developing a strong competitive streak is the surest way to lower your times.

The Final Surge

Once you pass the **five mile mark**, you can start thinking about making a final surge before the finish. If you are feeling strong, that final surge should come early rather than late. There's no sense in waiting until you see the finish line to begin picking up your pace. Everyone, no matter how strong or weak they're feeling, can surge a bit at the very end. The advantage comes from being able to pick up the pace well before the six mile mark and the final few hundred yards.

I like to think about how I'm going to make my move before actually doing it. You have to get yourself mentally and physically prepared for that final surge. There's no point in being able to surge ahead only for ten seconds, and then tire and fall back to a pace slower than what you were running before the surge.

The final push is not a sprint. You want to pick up your pace, but remember this not the final hundred yards of the race.

"Rest up" before making your move by tucking yourself behind another runner for about 30 seconds. During those 30 seconds, think about what you have to do. It helps to visualize your move right before you make it.

Start that final surge off fast and then worry about trying to sustain it for as long as possible. Mentally, it will really break the hopes of your fellow competitors if you are able to pass them effortlessly. If you are able to quickly pass them, and then not falter too much, it's highly unlikely that you will have to worry about those guys coming back to catch you at the very end of the race.

Unless the weather is quite warm, in the 80s or higher, do not stop for water during the race. Under normal weather conditions, anyone in good running shape should be able to race 6.2 miles without needing water. Your performance will not be affected as long as you drink plenty of water in the 24 hours prior to the race. If you have already gotten in the habit of stopping for water, you might as well continue doing it. It can, however, cause you to lose your rhythm at an important point in a competitive race.

---

5 THINGS TO REMEMBER: 10-K RACING

1. *Warm-up prior to the start of the race.*
2. *Get off to a strong start.*
3. *Run in a pack: let others help you keep the pace.*
4. *Don't wait for the very end to make your final push.*
5. *Run the day after racing.*

---

6. MARATHON TRAINING

The marathon is the ultimate test for the serious long distance runner. It takes a tremendous amount of stamina, desire and toughness to complete a marathon. It takes even more to train for one.

The secret to running a successful marathon is rigorous training. The weather on race day, the food you eat just prior to the race, your mental and physical state the week before, or even the amount of water you drink during the marathon, will not significantly affect your performance if you are not properly trained.

The toughest challenge you face is surviving the months of serious training leading up to the marathon. The first twenty miles of a marathon will be relatively easy, and the last six will not break you, if you bring months of disciplined training to the starting line.

PRE-MARATHON TRAINING: BUILDING A BASE

Not even Alberto Salazar in his prime could start training for a marathon from scratch. Even he required a foundation, a base. The marathon is an equal opportunity endeavor. None of us inherits the stamina and strength needed to run a solid marathon. We all have to work for it. Some of us may reap more from our efforts than others, but natural talent will not enable any runner to get through the twenty-first mile as fast as the first.

Starting your training in good physical condition is the first step towards running a successful marathon. You need a solid base on which to build. Without this foundation, you are bound to run into trouble during the high intensity period of your training when you must increase both the quality and the length of your runs. Your recent running history will define what qualifies as a solid base.

Example 1: Sue - Making the Jump to the Marathon

Sue is going to be running her first marathon. Over the past few years, she has consistently run three to four days a week, averaging about four miles a run. During her college years, she ran more, but she no longer has as much time to devote to her favorite sport.

Overall, Sue is in pretty good shape. She maintains a solid 7:30 to 8:00 minute pace during her runs. It's early May, and she has decided to enter the New York Marathon, six months away at the beginning of November. Her goal is to finish the marathon in about four hours, which translates into a pace of just over nine minutes per mile.

First, Sue has to make the change from running every other day to running six days a week. This is usually the hardest adjustment for a new marathoner to make. You no longer have the luxury of taking days off due to bad weather, or a busy work schedule. You can't skip the days when you just feel too lazy or too tired. It's critical to get yourself motivated to go out and run virtually every day. Gone are the times of taking a day off simply because you ran the day before. You are still allowed one day of rest a week, but you may not be able to plan ahead what day that will be, given all the minor uncontrollable events that come up during our daily lives.

If you fall into Sue's category, you should not try to make this adjustment from running every other day to every day over night. Give yourself one to two months of transition time. Don't worry about attempting to increase the distance or the pace of your runs during this period. That will come later. *The important thing is to get both your body and mind conditioned to getting out there almost every day of the week.*

Once the six day comfort level is reached, the next step is adding one run a week that goes about two miles beyond the four miles a day you're accustomed to running. This will allow your legs, as well as the rest of your body, some time to begin building up the strength they will need for the more rigorous training that lies ahead. It also helps mentally to get yourself conditioned to running for a serious 45-50 minutes, rather than a more leisurely half an hour. After about a month, add another longer run to your weekly schedule.

The process of building a base lasts about three months. By early August, three months before the New York Marathon, Sue has put together a solid base. Now she's ready for some serious marathon training. Over the prior three months, Sue increased her mileage from an average of about fifteen to close to thirty miles per week. She now considers her old four mile run as an easy day of training. She has also become comfortable with doing two longer runs a week, each lasting 50-55 minutes and covering six to seven miles.

TABLE 5: SUE'S PRE-MARATHON BASE TRAINING SCHEDULE - TYPICAL BASE TRAINING WEEK

	M	T	W	Th	F	S	Su
Month 1	4-5	3-4	off	4-5	3-4	off	4-5
Month 2	4-5	3-4	off	6	3-4	off	4-5
Month 3	4-5	6-7	3-4	off	4-5	6-7	3-4

Example 2: Randy - the 3:30 to 3:40 Marathoner

Randy has already completed a marathon in just under four hours. He decided to run that marathon only two months before the race, and set what he considered a modest goal of finishing just under four hours. Prior to training for his first marathon, Randy had been running approximately 25 miles a week and had participated in occasional 10-K races on the weekends.

Randy's first marathon experience went well. He felt comfortable throughout the race. He was able to maintain a consistent pace. He even completed the second half of the marathon a bit faster than the first half. With this experience under his belt, Randy feels he is capable of running a faster time, and is prepared to handle a more demanding training schedule leading up to the race.

Randy wants to take the time to train for his next marathon more seriously. He realizes that a greater commitment to training is likely to yield a significant improvement in his time. Randy's goal now is to finish the race in a time between 3:30 and 3:40, which translates into a pace of over eight minutes per mile, but under eight and a half. Like Sue, Randy plans to run a marathon that is still six months away, and will need some of that time to work on building a base. But, unlike Sue, Randy is already conditioned to running six days a week as part of his normal running routine.

Increasing his weekly mileage during the base training period to 35-40 miles a week from the past routine of 25 or 30 miles is the most important adjustment Randy has to make. In the past, he considered running 30 miles to be a big week. Now, he has to get his body used to the extra mileage. It's important, because once he hits the more intense training phase, he will have to handle about twenty more miles a week.

If you fall into Randy's category, give yourself some time to make the transition to the higher weekly mileage. Start thinking about preparing for your next marathon six months before the race. This allows you up to three months to work on your base training and to get comfortable with the higher weekly mileage.

Continue to Take One Day Off Per Week

This break serves two purposes. *First*, it gives your entire body an extra twenty-four hours to recover from the increased pounding and the strain to your legs muscles. *Second*, and equally important, it acts as a safety valve. The day off makes it less likely you will suffer from mental burn-out as you increase the amount of time you spend running each day.

About a month after you begin your pre-marathon base training, start thinking about picking out one day a week for a longer run. By this time, your average run should be about six miles in length, with some days ending up a mile or two longer or shorter depending on how you feel. Now, target one day a week for what should start out as an eight mile run, and increase this run to 10 or 11 miles by the end of your three month base training period. When you are three months away from race day you should have established two important running milestones that will put you in a good position to successfully complete the more intense marathon training that lies ahead:

Milestone One: *both your mind and body are accustomed to running substantial mileage week in and week out.*

Milestone Two: *you have begun to master the long run.* The 10 to 12 mile run you are able to do on a weekly base of only 35-40 miles is as difficult as the 20 mile run you will do at the peak of your marathon training.

There is nothing that lies ahead that will be more difficult than what you have already achieved. This should boost your confidence level as you enter the beginning phase of the three months of actual marathon training.

TABLE 6: RANDY'S PRE-MARATHON BASE TRAINING SCHEDULE - TYPICAL BASE TRAINING WEEK						
	M	**T**	**W**	**Th**	**F**	**S**	**Su**
Month 1	5-6	5-6	3-4	6-7	5-6	3-4	off
Month 2	5-6	5-6	8	3-4	6-7	5-6	off
Month 3	5-6	5-6	10-11	3-4	5-6	6-7	off

Example 3: The More Advanced Marathoner
More advanced marathon runners need not be pre-occupied with taking time to develop a pre-marathon base training schedule. Runners in this category are women capable of running under 3:20 and men who can run somewhere close to a time of three hours. In most cases, these runners' routine training gives them a sufficient base from which to train for a marathon. Their typical weekly

mileage will range somewhere between 40 and 50 miles. If you fall into this category, it is not necessary to set aside additional time before the marathon to work on your base training.

MARATHON TRAINING

Once you have established a base, the fun part begins – the actual training for the marathon. Ideally, set aside three months for the serious marathon training. If three months before the race you feel you have not developed a solid enough base, it's better to spend an extra two or three weeks on base training rather than jump under-trained into the more intensive marathon schedule. Getting through the marathon training is tough enough under the best conditions. It's nearly impossible if you don't enter into it with both your body and mind in top form.

Recently, a friend of mine reached the three month point before his marathon and faced this dilemma. Although he was steadily increasing his mileage, he still had not put together a solid base. So we pushed back his training schedule three weeks. He was in far better shape only doing nine solid weeks of marathon training and doing it well, than burning out his body weeks before the marathon in an attempt to stick to a prescribed timetable.

It's always better to err on the side of caution and arrive at the starting line of the marathon a bit under-trained than risk injury or burnout by trying to do too much too fast. Getting through the training in relatively good shape will make the marathon itself a relatively easy exercise. The bad news is that the training leading up to the marathon is really going to test your mettle. The good news is running the actual marathon won't be nearly as tough.

Since the proper training for the marathon prepares you so well for the race, someone like my friend, Andy, who ends up condensing his training by 10 or 20 percent, will still be in line to reach his goal of breaking four hours. He may have to struggle a bit towards the end of the race to get there, but the chances are good that he will make it.

Sure, it would have been better if he had put in twelve solid weeks instead of nine. It might have enabled him to meet his four hour goal more easily or, better yet, break it, which would make him feel a lot more confident in preparing for his next marathon.

The point is this: you must show as much if not more respect for the training leading up to the marathon as you do for the marathon itself. Three months is about the right amount of time, as long as you are going into it ready.

---

5 THINGS TO REMEMBER: MARATHON TRAINING

1. *Develop a solid base before starting your marathon training.*
2. *Err on the side of caution over excess.*
3. *Break your training into three distinct periods:*
   • Build-up • High-intensity • Tapering
4. *Master the long run.*
5. *Take it easy on your recovery days.*

Back to Example 1: The Four Hour Training Guide

In my view, it's the marathoners who end up running around four hours who have the most heart. One spring a few years back, I had the opportunity to run two marathons, one competitively, the other four weeks later to help a friend out. The first one I ran in the 2:30s, which I was fairly pleased with, though I was hoping to break 2:30. In the second race, the Boston Marathon, my goal was to keep my friend on course to reach her four hour goal, which she did.

The runners I was with in the first race were fairly homogeneous – male, in their twenties or early thirties, competitive runners in college, and were probably a bit too anal. We were considered naturals at running, having been doing it well for a long time, and each of us looked like we should gain at least twenty pounds. We all ran good times. But instead of feeling good about our time, most of us sulked afterwards, thinking we could have done better. We were the running equivalent of over-educated yuppies, always trying to get one step ahead of everyone else in our careers.

Hanging out with the four hour marathoners in the second race was a lot more inspiring. I always enjoy being at the finish line of a marathon at around the four hour mark and watching people complete the big race. These finishers are the real heart and soul of the running populace. Their ages, shapes, and running experiences vary, but none of them take finishing a marathon in four hours for granted. And most have to really fight to get there. They are out there hitting the pavement giving it all they've got for four hours.

Phase 1: Increasing your Mileage

The twelve weeks of training for the marathon consist of three distinct periods. In the first phase, lasting about five weeks, the focus is on **increasing your weekly mileage level**. Think of it as an expansion upon your base training. During base training, the goal was to get your body accustomed to a higher but constant weekly mileage level of 25 to 30 miles. Now, you need to get yourself used to running through a period in which the weekly mileage steadily increases. Over a relatively short period of time, your weekly mileage will rise from about 30 to approximately 45 miles.

Through this phase, as well as during the rest of your marathon training, allow yourself one day off per week. The day off and the easy runs during the week (your recovery days) are as important as your longer and harder runs. These days will enable you to remain fresh for your higher intensity and longer runs, making them more productive. An easy day now should now be considered a run of four miles.

At the beginning of your training, you might be tempted to run a bit harder or longer on an easy day, since all that base training has left you in great shape. Don't let yourself fall into this trap. Save your energy for the other runs of the week. It means a whole lot more to be able to say you were able to get through your first couple of 10 or 12 mile runs smoothly, than being able to add an extra mile or knock off 30 seconds per mile to your four mile run.

The temptation to run hard on the easy days should not be a problem once you start to pile up the longer runs. Your leg muscles will begin to feel a bit more strained and tight on the days following the longer runs, which will preclude you from wanting to run hard on a recovery day. Instead, you will begin to see these days as a great opportunity to work out the kinks in your legs in order to be ready for the next long run.

Let's turn now to the more intensive days of training during the week. **First, set aside two days for longer runs**. Consider these runs as an effort to steadily expand upon the long runs you began during base training. Then, the purpose was to get accustomed to runs lasting six to seven miles in length. Now, you will begin with an eight mile run that will jump in distance over a month's time to about 12 to 13 miles.

For the first week or two, both runs should be about the same distance, but after that, one of the runs should be longer than the other. At the end of this period, you will be doing two longer runs a week, but only during one will you go as far as 13 miles. The other should remain about ten miles.

In the beginning, these long runs will really test your mettle. The first ten miler might be especially tough to get through. The key is to just get through these first few runs; they will soon get easier. Don't worry about maintaining a consistent pace throughout these longer runs at the beginning. If you have to slow down a bit in the middle or towards the end of the run, that's okay; just don't stop – unless something is really bothering you.

For example, running seven miles, then stopping and walking for five minutes, then going on to run another four miles, is not the equivalent for training purposes of running 11 miles. All you have really done is run seven miles, far short of the 10 you needed to do. The extra four you put in after you stopped, while it's better than throwing in the towel completely, is fairly meaningless for purposes of improving your endurance.

Building Mental Toughness

It's not just for endurance reasons that you should hang in there during those early long runs when your legs feel especially tight and tired, or your stomach cramps up a bit. As crucial as it is to finish these runs in order to improve your endurance, it's just as important to get through these runs for the purposes of building up your mental toughness.

Probably the toughest hurdle to get over for someone new to the marathon experience is a mental one. It's telling yourself on one of those more trying days that, "Alright, I'm not feeling so great, or enjoying this right now, but I can get through it, and in another few miles I'll be done and will feel a lot better about being able to complete today's run." It's about compensating for a touch of physical discomfort with a strong mental outlook, instead of letting your physcial condition dictate how you feel mentally.

Like most things in life, the ability to maintain a strong mental outlook becomes easier with experience. You will see this as you successfully complete the first few long runs. It also gives you the confidence to take on greater endeavors – like the 15-20 mile runs that lie ahead.

GETTING THROUGH THE DOWN DAYS

To use a baseball analogy, it's a lot like a day when a great pitcher like Roger Clemens does not have his best stuff, but his confidence, poise, and competitive nature keep him from giving up so many runs that he has to be taken out of the game early. He may struggle in the early innings and give up a few runs, but he is able to regain his composure and pitch six or seven innings and keep his team in the ballgame. Getting through those "down" days keeps you on schedule to achieve your goal.

Keep in mind that an added sense of confidence is not the only benefit you receive from being mentally tough. It's also a tool for achieving a more important goal: getting yourself in significantly better physical shape. You may not feel the actual benefit that day, or even that week, but you're getting stronger. So, instead of letting an off day physically get you down mentally, your mental toughness yields positive physical dividends.

One of the most important factors for gauging success is how well you're able to get through those days when you feel less than 100 percent. That's more important than how well you're able to get through the tough workouts on days when you feel great.

The "Solid Six" Day

So far, we have covered six days of the week - the off day, three recovery days and the two longer days, which leaves us one more day to think about. On this day, the goal should be just to get in a good quality run of about six miles – and by quality I mean maintaining a solid pace throughout the run. Call it your **solid six** day. The pace during this run should be faster than either your pace on the recovery days or the long runs.

It's important that your legs are given a day to run a bit harder than the usual steady pace of the other days. It keeps you from becoming terminally locked into one pace of running, thereby limiting the capacity of your muscles to offer you greater leg speed. The pace on these runs should not vary dramatically from your other runs. Increasing the pace about 30 seconds per mile is sufficient.

Structuring Your Week

Now that all the days of the week are covered, it's time to think about how to structure your typical week of running. First, it should not come as a surprise that I recommend doing a recovery run on the two days following the long runs. If, for instance, you are planning to do your long runs on Monday and Thursday, make Tuesday and Friday easy days.

Some runners are inclined to believe they need to rest the day after a long run and to take it as their day off. Don't do this. It's important to follow up an intense day of running, whether a long run or a race, with an easy day of running, as opposed to a day off. Running the day after helps reduce the degree of lingering soreness or feeling of tightness in your leg muscles that develop after a more strenuous workout. This should reduce the amount of time it takes for your legs to feel fresh again. By taking a day off after a long run, you are making your leg muscles wait an extra twenty-four hours for the opportunity to loosen up and work out the soreness.

Take your day off two days after the longest run of the week. Make your first day back after an off day a relatively easy day. This gives you a nice period of recovery after the longest run of the week, since the next three days will be comprised of an easy day, an off day, and another easy day. Then you'll be ready for your first long run of the week, followed by another easy day, and then the "solid six" run, the day you'll concentrate on maintaining a strong pace. Then, three days after the first long run of the week, it's time for the other long run.

A TYPICAL WEEK IN PHASE ONE
- **Monday**: *easy four miles*
- **Tuesday**: *longer run of eight miles*
- **Wednesday**: *easy four miles*
- **Thursday**: *solid six miles*
- **Friday**: *ten - twelve miles*
- **Saturday**: *easy four*
- **Sunday**: *off*

Refer to the table on page 59 for the entire suggested twelve-week advanced runner's training schedule. Many runners like to save their longest run of the week for the weekend. That's fine. The important thing is keeping the schedule the same in terms of the type of run you do each day of the week, from week to week.

By the end of this first phase of training, which takes about five weeks, two goals should be reached. First, you have conditioned yourself to increasing your mileage from week to week to the point where its up to somewhere in the range of 40 to 45 miles. Second, and more specifically, you are capable of running 12 miles comfortably one day during the week.

You should also be thinking about your form. I recommend you read the section on *Quality Runs & Concentrating on Form,* which begins on page 88.

Phase 2: Mastering the Long Run

Just as the first phase of training built upon your base training, this second phase, **lasting four weeks**, expands upon your achievements in the first phase. While the training during the next four weeks will become more intense, highlighted by a twenty mile run, it should not be more difficult to get through than what you have already accomplished to this point.

Many inexperienced runners make the mistake of getting totally preoccupied with getting in a couple of 20 mile runs before the marathon, and do not concentrate enough on the rest of their training. This makes their twenty mile runs such an exhausting experience that it leaves them with little energy left for the actual marathon. This should not happen to you, given the steady progress you will make by following a gradual training schedule.

This is not to suggest that you will now be able to breeze through all or any of your 15 to 20 mile runs. You are still likely to struggle a bit through some of them, but, because of all the solid running you have already done, these runs will not break you. Instead, they will help make you a stronger runner on race day.

The First Week

Over the course of the next four weeks you will be running four important long runs, **beginning with a 15 miler** in the first week. The rest of your first week's schedule should remain the same.

This 15 mile run may end up being the most challenging run of your entire marathon training. Making the jump from 12 to 15 miles is likely to be more difficult than the increase you make the following week to 18 miles, or even the 20 miler you will do the week after – if you can run 18, you can do 20. Don't worry too much about how well you run the first 15 miler, since you will be entering new territory in terms of your long distance experience. Just get through it.

The Second Week

On the following week, **increase the long run to 18 miles**. Get yourself psyched up for this one. More than any other long run during your training, you must combine quantity with quality on this one. This is not a run that you want to end up struggling to get through.

It's important to run the 18 miler well, because if you do, it will give you the confidence to take on the 20 mile run the following week. In order to help ensure that the 18 mile run goes smoothly, limit your other long run of the week to about 8 miles. Limit all the recovery day runs to four miles. All your energy for the week should be focused on the 18 miler.

What makes the 18 miler a quality run? The consistency of the pace you achieve for each mile, not the overall time of the run. You want to end the run at the same pace you started it, as well as maintaining that pace during the miles in between. At this point in your training, you should be able to keep yourself on track in terms of maintaining a consistent pace. Even when fatigue hits your legs and other body parts, you should now be able to maintain that steady pace.

The Third Week
After completing the 18 miler, you will be ready for **the big 20 mile run**. How well you do it is less important than just getting out there and completing the run without any major mishaps. In other words, don't worry if you have to struggle a bit to finish it.

This is the point in your training where your legs are likely to feel the most tired. The first 20 mile run is not an easy experience. It should be a tough run. If your legs are not completely exhausted at the end of the run, you have not been training hard enough.

After completing the run, avoid this line of thought: "I could barely finish 20 miles, how am I ever going to do 26?" Keep in mind that you ran 20 miles on tired legs at the peak of your training. It will take some time before you will be able to reap the benefits of all this high mileage training.

But on race day, your legs will be well rested and you'll have the benefits of all that hard training kicking in. Actually, your thinking should be more along the lines of: "If I can do 20 miles now running alone and on tired legs, doing six more in a race with thousands of other runners with fresh legs should not be that difficult."

The Fourth Week

Now, you have only one week left of the second phase of training. This week should include **a long run of about 18 miles**. In terms of quality, this run should probably fall somewhere in between your first 18 miler and the 20 mile run you did last week. It all depends on how you feel that day.

If your legs feel good don't hesitate to push yourself, since this run is the last real long run you will do before the marathon. This will also be the last week of running high mileage. At the end of this week, the marathon should be only three weeks away.

Longer Run Checklist: Maintain an Average Pace

Your **average pace per mile** during the long runs should be close to the pace you plan to run the marathon – within 15-30 seconds. *In the case of a four hour marathon, this should be about a nine minute per mile pace.* It's okay if your first 15 miler and the 20 mile run are a bit slower, but try to get your two 18 mile runs a little under the nine mile per minute pace. Remember not to start out too fast. What seems somewhat slow at the start will end up feeling just about right as you get further along the run.

Drink Up!

As you do these longer runs, don't forget to drink enough liquids during the day to guard against dehydration. It's a good idea to drink a few extra glasses of water on the day of the long run. In order to avoid cramping up during the run, try to get most of the water down at least an hour before the run.

Don't drink more than about a half glass of water a half-hour prior to the run. Once the runs start to get over twelve miles or so, don't hestitate during the run to stop once for a brief water break. Try to limit it to one stop, or maybe two, during the 20 mile run, unless you are running on an exceedingly hot or humid day.

Some people like to run with water bottles attached to a belt that can be purchased at most running/athletic stores. That's fine with me, as long as you don't find the belt too cumbersome. Better still, choose a route where you will pass a working water fountain, or if your run involves more than one loop, you can make a quick stop at your house. Keep the water stops to minimum, since each break for water involves taking a detour from your training route.

WATER BASICS

Remember: drink plenty of water during the hours before the run; a modest amount leading up to the run, and as little as possible during the run – but do not hestitate to stop at least once. The rule on drinking water will change for the day of the race, but we'll get to that later.

Don't Always Run on the Same Side of the Street

It's important to be alert to alternating the side of the street you run on during the longer outings. It's common to get into the habit of always running on the left side of the street in order to keep a watch for on-coming traffic. Generally this is not a bad idea, since getting hit by a car could put a serious damper on your training! But always running on the left side of the street puts an added strain on the lower left part of your leg. This occurs because just about all streets slope downward near the curb, and therefore you end up exerting more weight on the left side of your body than if you were running on a flat surface.

This is not a concern if you always have a trail or the sidewalk to use. If you are on the street, choose a portion of the run where the traffic is not heavy and run on the right side of the road. You do not have to split the two sides evenly, just be sure that a few miles of a long run are done on the right side.

Don't Overdo It!

As I mentioned earlier, it's always better to go into the marathon a bit under-trained than risk burnout or injury from either over-training or attempting to compensate too much for lost time. If, for example, something comes up that keeps you from doing one of your long runs, do not try to do two the next week, or push your entire schedule back a week, causing you to run too far so close to the day of the race. Instead, give yourself two weeks time to do what you had planned to do over the next week, and drop a week from your training schedule.

Let's say, for example, you get a nasty cold or the flu, putting you out of action for the week when you are slated to run the 20 miler. Come back the next week and do the 20 mile run. Skip the 18 mile run you would have done the week after the 20 miler and move onto the next week of training in order to get back on schedule. The timing of when you do the runs in the course of the overall training schedule is as important as the length of the runs. Stay flexible about your schedule.

The rest of your runs during the second phase should remain about the same in distance and intensity as they were during the first phase. You might want to extend your first easy run of the week a mile or two following your day off. The other long run should remain about ten miles in length. Remember, as discussed earlier, to scale back these runs a bit for the week of your first 18 mile run. See the table on page 84 for more details.

Upon completion of the second phase of training, you have really reached a milestone in your running career. You will likely never face another challenge in your running career as demanding as these four weeks. It's tougher than the marathon itself, or any more advanced training schedule you may attempt to do in the future. Now you can take on either of those endeavors with a lot more experience under your belt.

Even though the race itself is still three weeks away, it's only natural to a feel a great sense of accomplishment. Go out and celebrate a little!

Phase 3: Tapering the Mileage

Compared to what you just went through, the last three weeks of training should be a piece of cake, especially when you take into consideration the great shape you'll be in. During this period, your weekly mileage will drop considerably, going from about 40 miles to the low twenties for the week leading up to the marathon.

Begin to significantly reduce your mileage. Why? *First*, once you get within three weeks of the race, you do not have enough to time to reap the positive benefits acquired from the endurance-building long runs. *Second*, you want to have your legs, the rest of your body, and your mind well rested and fresh for the race.

Many first-time marathoners make the mistake of training too hard and long in the final weeks leading up to the race. They fear that everything they have gained from their training will be lost by the time they run the marathon unless they continue with the high mileage. But going out and doing a long and hard run a week or two prior to the marathon is more likely to hinder than help your race day performance. All those months of serious training will not whither away as a result of tapering off during the final weeks. That tremendous reservoir of endurance you have created over the last few months will not recede before race day.

Should every run be short and easy during the final three weeks? Of course not. You still have to keep your leg muscles accustomed to doing longer distances, but they just don't have to be pushed to the point of fatigue.

Week One of Phase 3

You still need to include **one long run of about 15 miles** during the first week of Phase Three. If your legs are feeling good, try to maintain a moderate and consistent pace. This will be the last run you'll do over ten miles in length before the marathon.

The other "long" run of the week will be limited to six or seven miles. The rest of the week should remain about the same as what you were doing during the last month. If your legs are feeling a bit tight leading up to the long run, you might want to take a mile off your solid six run.

Week Two of Phase 3

Week Two follows the same pattern except for **the long run, which drops down to ten miles**. At this point, you should be able to run a solid ten miles with ease. In fact, all your runs during this week should feel good. By now, your legs have recovered from all the tough running from the preceding month.

You may even have to hold yourself back at times during this week, since you will combine a relatively light training schedule with a body that is in excellent running shape. These runs ought to be quality runs, but remember: you want to save most of your energy for the day of the race. Your total mileage for this week should fall in the range of 33-35 miles.

SLEEP SMART!

*In terms of **sleep**, your sweetest dreams should be two nights before the race, not the night before. Lack of sleep usually does not catch up to you for twelve to twenty-four hours. Limit the amount of sleep the night before the race to no more than six or seven hours. This should not be too difficult to do since you're likely be pretty wound up and you'll have to get up early the next morning to eat well before the race. You do not want to wake up the morning of the race feeling groggy from sleeping too long. Try to get in a good eight to nine hours of sleep on the two or three days prior to the night before the marathon.*

The Third & Final Week of Phase 3

Now, you are ready for the final week of training. The whole point of this week is to run just enough so that your legs remain loose for the race. Take an extra day off, and limit your longest runs to six miles.

If, for example, the marathon is on Sunday, run four to five miles on Monday and Wednesday, take Thursday off, and limit your runs on Friday and Saturday to four miles or less. On Saturday, I would only run an easy twenty minutes or so, whatever it takes to get your legs warmed up enough to get in a good stretch afterwards. Your mileage for the entire week will only be in the low 20's. By the end of this week, you should be itching to run long and hard, given how light your final couple of weeks of training have been. It's always a good idea to eat some **pasta** or other foods high in carbohydrates the night before the big race. Eat food that your body is used to digesting. Get in a good meal the night before, since you will have only a light breakfast the next morning – but don't overdo it. Drink plenty of water during the forty-eight hours prior to the big run.

Tables 7 and 8 lay out a training schedule, as discussed in the preceding pages, for a four hour marathon.

	M	T	W	Th	F	S	Su
TABLE 7: 12-WEEK, FOUR HOUR MARATHON TRAINING SCHEDULE							
Week 1	4	7-8	4	5	8	4	off
Week 2	4	7-8	4	5-6	8-9	4	off
Week 3	4	7-8	4	6	10-11	4	off
Week 4	4	8	4	6	10-11	4	off
Week 5	5	8	4	6	12-13	4	off
Week 6	5-6	10	4	6	15	4	off
Week 7	4	7-8	4	6	18	4	off
Week 8	5	8-10	4	6	20	4	off
Week 9	5-6	8	4	6	18	4	off
Week 10	4	6-7	4	5-6	15	4	off
Week 11	4	6-7	4	5	10	4	off
Week 12	4	6	4-5	off	4	2-3	race

	M	**T**	**W**	**Th**	**F**	**S**	**Su**
TABLE 8: 9-WEEK CONDENSED FOUR HOUR TRAINING SCHEDULE							
Week 1	4	7-8	4	5-6	10	4	off
Week 2	4	7-8	4	6	10	4	off
Week 3	5-6	8	4	6	12	4	off
Week 4	6	10	4	6	15	4	off
Week 5	6	8	4	6	18	4	off
Week 6	6	8-10	4	6	20	4	off
Week 7	6	10	4	6	15	4	off
Week 8	4	6-7	4	5-6	10	4	off
Week 9	4	6	off	6	4	2-3	race

Back to Example 2: Running in the 3:30's

As mentioned earlier in the pre-marathon section, getting accustomed to running roughly 35 to 40 miles a week is necessary before beginning the twelve weeks of marathon training. To a large degree, the weekly schedule follows the same pattern as the four hour guide. The focus is still on steadily increasing the distance of one run a week, allowing yourself a couple of easy recovery days a week, and concentrating one day per week on pace. You still even get to take one day off each week.

The difference is that the long runs start sooner, and therefore occur more often over the course of the twelve weeks; the recovery day runs are a couple of miles longer; and the pace runs become more demanding. In other words, there are no shortcuts to success.

There are no special secrets. In order to get your time down to the 3:30s, you must run longer and harder.

Like the four hour training schedule, the twelve weeks are divided into three periods: the build-up phase, the high mileage phase, and the tapering off period. Now, however, the build-up phase is shorter — lasting four weeks — and an additional week is added to the high mileage period, making it a total of five weeks. The tapering off phase remains the same at three weeks.

Your weekly mileage at the beginning of the 12 weeks will be in the mid-40's, rising to 60 miles at the peak of training, and then falling to under 30 miles in the week leading up to the race. Your goal is to be able to run the marathon at a pace of about eight minutes per mile.

Phase 1: The Build Up

In this first phase, which lasts four weeks, the focus is on getting your body conditioned to higher and steadily increasing weekly mileage. Consider it to be an extension of your base training. The rise in mileage over this period is not as steep, in absolute terms, relative to someone following the four hour training schedule. Their mileage increases 50 percent, from about 30 miles to 45. While your buildup will be less precipitous, beginning at about 40 miles and rising to the low 50's, it's accomplished over less time and with more intensity.

Surging to Quick Tempo Heaven!

One aspect of this first phase that differs significantly from your prior base training period is the introduction of the **quick tempo run** (the *fartlek*, discussed earlier) to the weekly schedule. Again, the idea behind it is to choose distinct intervals during a run to surge for a limited time period. By surge, I mean to pick up speed, but not to the point of sprinting. The intent is to run harder than a pace you feel comfortable with, but not so hard that you to feel winded at the end of the interval.

After completing the surge, it's important not to slow down beyond the comfortable pace you were maintaining before the surge. It defeats the whole purpose of the run if you begin to slow down beyond your normal pace between surges. One of the purposes of these runs is to build up your cardiovascular capacity by adjusting your breathing to the increase in heart rate that results from the surge. If you slow down too much, you are letting your heart off the hook.

It is not just your heart and cardiovascular system that benefits from these quick tempo runs. They are also good for your legs. It's important that your legs are given a day to run a bit harder than the usual steady pace of the other days. It keeps you from becoming locked into one pace and also limits the ability of your leg muscles to offer you greater speed.

On your first quick tempo run, use the first two miles as a warm-up. The pace should be relaxed and easy. Once you are about two miles into the run, begin doing surges for about two minutes every five minutes. Run hard for two minutes, maintain your normal training pace for five, and then do another surge for two minutes. Repeat the process until you have done four two minute surges. Finish up, as you started, with an easy warm-down of two miles.

In the second week, I recommend repeating the work-out of the first week. It will take a bit of time to adjust to these quick tempo runs if you have never done them before. Wait until the third week to increase the amount and duration of the surges. **In weeks three and four** of the build-up phase, increase the duration of the surges to three minutes every six minutes, and also raise the total to five. As in the first two weeks, continue to start and end the run with an easy two miles.

Your Long Run

Besides the thrill of *fartleking*, the other key run of the week is **the long run.** You are probably already comfortable with doing a 10 to 12 mile run once a week by the time you start this first phase of marathon training. Start the first week with a run of about 12 miles. Try to add a mile or two to the run during the following week. The goal is to feel comfortable with a long run of 15 miles by the end of the four week build-up period.

The Importance of Easing Up

Ease up on your training a few days a week at this point. Through this phase, as well as during the rest of your training, take one day off a week. The day off combined with the easy runs during the week, which I like to think of as recovery days, are as important as your longer and harder runs in terms of making your marathon experience a success. These recovery days will enable you to remain fresh for higher intensity and longer runs, and thereby make them more productive. Limit your easy runs to five to six miles, and schedule them on the days following the long run and the quick tempo run.

At the beginning of your training, you might be tempted to run a bit harder or longer on an easy day, since all that base training has left you in great shape. Don't fall into this trap. Save your energy for the other runs of the week. It means a whole lot more to be able to get through your first couple of 12 to 15 mile runs smoothly than being able to add an extra couple of miles or knock off 30 seconds per mile during your six mile run.

Quality Runs & Concentrating on Form

So far, we have covered five days of the week - the day off, two recovery days, the quick tempo run and the long run. That leaves us with two more days to cover. On these days, do **quality runs** of seven to eight miles. Start out at seven miles during the first few weeks, and then try to raise it to eight miles for the following week. I define quality as being be able to maintain a solid, consistent pace throughout the run. Run a bit faster than the easy pace of a recovery day, but do not push yourself beyond a pace you can sustain comfortably.

These runs offer an opportunity to concentrate on **your running form**. It is a good idea to take time to be conscious about maintaining a fluid running style throughout your runs. This is not to suggest that you should think about changing the way in which you run. All of us to some degree have a distinct way of running, which for better or worse we should not try to change. You risk opening yourself up to injury, not to mention a lot of frustration by attempting to change your natural running stride.

During my cross country days in college, I had a teammate who always sounded like he was having an acute asthma attack because his breathing was so strained by the way he ran. He had the habit of swinging his arms so far across his chest that it put so much pressure on his rib cage that it affected his breathing. I tried to get him to swing his arms forward instead of across his chest. Unfortunately, the advice I gave him did not yield a positive result. He ended up running slower because he became preoccupied in attempting to run in a style that was unfamiliar to him. He forgot about concentrating on running hard. So he went back to sounding like a walrus and the team was better for it.

The purpose of taking form into consideration is to get yourself conscious about not deviating from your best personal style. I like to tell people to pretend that at any moment throughout the middle of the run you may be photographed for a running magazine, so you want to look your strongest. But not for reasons of narcissism; the better your form, the more efficiently you'll run. The more efficiently you run, the less energy you use to maintain the same pace. And the less energy you use to maintain your usual pace, the more energy you'll have. In other words, maintaining good form enables you to run faster when you are feeling good, and keeps you from slowing down when you are tired.

It's when fatigue starts setting in that it is especially important not to let your form slip. You can waste a substantial amount of energy by starting to slump over too much, shortening your stride, lowering your head, or deviating in other ways from your usual stride as a long run grinds on. The more you concentrate on thinking about good form during the days you do the solid seven or eight, the more often you will be able to maintain it during the more demanding long and quick tempo runs. Spending time concentrating on your form will particularly come in handy on marathon day.

Structuring Your Week

Now that all the days of the week are covered, it's time to think about how to structure your typical week of running. As mentioned previously, do the easy recovery runs on the days following the long and quick tempo runs. Put a fair amount of space between your long run and quick tempo day. For example, if you plan to do your long run on Saturday, do the quick tempo or surge run on Wednesday, and make Sunday and Thursday your easy days.

Some runners are inclined to believe they need to rest the day after a long run, and take it as their day off. Don't do this. It is important to follow up an intense day of running with an easy day of running, as opposed to a day off. Running the day after helps to lessen the degree of lingering soreness and/or the tight feeling in your leg muscles that develops after a more strenuous workout. This should work to reduce the amount of time it takes for your legs to feel fresh again. By taking a day off after a long run, you are making your leg muscles wait an extra twenty-four hours for the opportunity to loosen up and work out the tightness.

Take your day off two days after the long run on Monday. Then follow the day off with one of the solid seven to eight mile runs, with the other occurring on Friday. This schedule offers you a nice recovery period after the long run, since the next three days will be comprised of an easy run, a day off, and a solid run of seven to eight miles.

A TYPICAL WEEK AT THE START OF YOUR MARATHON TRAINING:

- **Saturday** – *long run of 12-15 miles*
- **Sunday** – *easy five to six*
- **Monday** – *off*
- **Tuesday** – *solid seven*
- **Wednesday** – *quick tempo run*
- **Thursday** – *easy five to six*
- **Friday** – *solid seven*

See the table on page 84 for the entire suggested 12 week training schedule. It's up to you to decide which day to do each run. The important thing is to try to keep the schedule the same in terms of the type of run you do each day of the week, from week to week.

This first phase of your training lasts four weeks. By the end of it you will have reached two important goals: first, you've become acclimated to the quick tempo run, and second, you've conquered 15 miles without too much of a struggle. Your weekly mileage at the end of this period should be up to the low fifties.

Phase 2: High Mileage

Now you're ready for the big time. The training over the next five weeks will become more intense, highlighted by two 20 mile runs. Given the demands of maintaining a training schedule requiring 55 to 60 miles a week, this phase will test your running mettle even more than the marathon itself. Nevertheless, you should enter this period full of confidence. You are now in superb running shape from the prior weeks of build-up and base training.

Your Old Friend The Long Run

Gaining command of the long run is your goal over these five weeks. Unlike the four hour marathoner, whose primary purpose is to just get through a series of long runs, you must raise the quality up a notch for most of these runs. This is not to suggest that each one of the long runs has to break barriers. That's not the case.

For instance, the first twenty miler will probably not come easy. There will be runs in which your legs will not be in sync with the demands of the workout for that day. On those days, rely on your mental toughness to avoid easing up too much. But on most of the runs during this period, especially towards the end, you should feel strong. By the second twenty mile run, expect to break new ground.

During the **first two weeks**, make your long runs 18 miles. Try to maintain a per mile pace close to eight minutes. In **the third week**, increase the run to 20 miles. This run does not need to be pretty; you just need to get through it. You will be running 20 miles on tired legs at the peak of your training, so don't worry if your pace slows a bit on this day.

After completing the first 20 miler, avoid thinking: "I could barely do 20 miles under an eight-and-a-half minute pace, how am I ever going to do 26 miles averaging eight minutes per mile?" It will take some time before you reap the benefits of all this high mileage training. Remember, on race day your legs will be well rested, and the benefits from all that hard training will be kicking in. Your thinking should be more along the lines of: "If I can do 20 miles today, running alone on tired legs at an 8:30 pace, doing six miles more at a clip thirty seconds faster in a race with thousands of other runners should not be that difficult."

Easing Up

Ease up a bit the week after the first 20 mile run. Think of it as taking a vacation from your vacation. If you're having so much fun running so hard, rest up a bit before continuing with the adventure.

Shorten your long run to 15 miles and reduce the intensity of the quick tempo run to what you were doing in the early weeks of training. Repeat this light, quick tempo run in the week that follows. Cutting back this week and at the beginning of the next allows you to get your legs ready for the most important run prior to the marathon – the second 20 miler, which you'll do the following week.

While no single run prior to the marathon is going to determine your fate on race day, how well you do on the second 20 mile run, just over three weeks before the race, could mean a lot. Look at it as a great opportunity to get in one last long and intense run at the time when it will benefit you the most.

The Last 20 Miler

Once you get under three weeks, there is not enough time remaining to reap the positive benefits acquired from these endurance-building long runs. In the case of this last 20 miler, however, the stronger you make the run, the more you will have in the bank for race day. Don't start out trying to break a world record, but do try to maintain a consistent eight-minute-per-mile pace throughout the run. If you are feeling really good, finish the run a bit faster.

Phase Two Checklist

Keep the easy runs following the long and quick tempo runs at five to six miles during this phase. Similarly, keep the distance for the two solid runs at eight miles for the first three weeks, but shorten it a mile on the week before and during the second 20 miler. Also, continue to give yourself a day off two days after the long run.

During the long runs, be alert to alternating the side of the street you run on. It's common to get into the habit of always running on the left side of the street in order to keep a watch for on-coming traffic. Generally, this is not a bad idea, since getting hit by a car could put a serious damper on your training. But always running on the left side of the street puts an added strain on the lower left portion of your leg. This occurs, as mentioned earlier, because just about all streets slope downward near the curb, and therefore you end up exerting more weight on the left side of your body than if you were running on a flat surface.

Don't worry if you always have a trail or sidewalk to use. If you are on the street, choose a portion of the run where the traffic is not heavy, and run on the right side of the road. You do not have to split the two sides evenly, just ensure that a few miles of the long runs are done on the right side.

Again, it is always better to go into the marathon a bit under-trained than risk burnout or injury from over-training, or attempting to compensate too much for lost time. If something comes up that keeps you from doing one of your long runs, do not try to do two the following week, or to push your entire schedule back a week, causing you to run too far too close to the day of the marathon. Instead, give yourself two weeks time to accomplish what you had planned to do over the next week, and drop a week from your training schedule.

Upon completion of the high mileage phase, you will be in the best shape of your life. As stated earlier, running the marathon will not be nearly as difficult as what you have just accomplished over the past five weeks. With the marathon still three weeks away, go out and celebrate a little a bit. Training for and running a quality marathon are two great achievements. There is no rule stipulating that you cannot celebrate both.

Phase 3: Tapering the Mileage

Compared to what you just went through, the last weeks of training should be easy (especially when you take into consideration the great shape you will be in). During this final period, your weekly mileage falls from about 50 to under 30 miles.

It is important to begin to significantly reduce your mileage for two reasons. First, as mentioned previously, once you get within three weeks of the race, you do not have enough time to reap the benefits received from the endurance-building long runs. Second, you want to have your legs and the rest of your body, as well as your mind, well-rested and fresh for the race.

All those months of serious training will not whither away as a result of the tapering you do during these final three weeks. The tremendous reservoir of endurance that you have created over many months will continue to build over the last couple of weeks. This is not to suggest that every run during the final three weeks should be short and easy. You still must keep your leg muscles accustomed to doing longer distances, but they no longer have to be pushed to the point of serious fatigue. The first week still includes a long run of 16 miles, run at a solid pace as long as you feel that your legs have adequately recovered from your last 20 miler.

On the weekend one week before the marathon, take a long run of 12 miles. This will be your last run over ten miles before the marathon. During this week, move every run in your schedule up a day. For example, if you usually do your long run on Saturday and take Monday off, run the 12 miler on Friday and take Sunday off. By doing this, you are allowing more space between the day of the marathon and the last runs of any serious intensity.

The Final Week

Now, you are ready for your final week of training. Basically, the whole idea behind this final week is to just run enough so that your legs remain loose for the race. Assuming that the marathon is on Sunday, do a relatively easy tempo run on Monday, something along the lines of three two-minute surges every five minutes, with a ten minute warm-up and warm-down. Run an easy four to five on Tuesday and Friday. Do a solid seven on Wednesday, and take Thursday off. On Saturday, run for only twenty minutes or so, or whatever it takes to get your legs warmed up enough to get in a good stretch afterwards.

TABLE 9: 12 WEEK 3:30-3:40 MARATHON TRAINING SCHEDULE

	M	T	W	Th	F	S	Su
Week 1	off	7	srg	5-6	7	12	5-6
Week 2	off	7	srg	5-6	7	12-13	5-6
Week 3	off	7	srg	5-6	7	13-14	5-6
Week 4	off	8	srg	5-6	8	15	5-6
Week 5	off	8	srg	5-6	8	18	5-6
Week 6	off	8	srg	5-6	8	18	5-6
Week 7	off	8	srg	5-6	8	20	5-6
Week 8	off	7	srg	5-6	7	15	5-6
Week 9	off	7	srg	5-6	7	21	5-6
Week 10	off	7	srg	5-6	7	16	5-6
Week 11	off	6	srg	4-5	12	4-5	off
Week 12	srg*	4-5	7	off	4-5	2-3	race

Srg = surge
abbreviated surge workout: 3 two-minute surges every 5 minutes

In terms of sleep, the most important day to get a lot of it is two days before the race, not the night before. Lack of sleep usually does not catch up to you for twelve to twenty-four hours. In fact, you should limit the amount of sleep the night before to six or seven hours. You do not want to wake up the morining of the race feeling all groggy from sleeping too long. Try to get in a good eight to nine hours of sleep two to three days prior to the night before the marathon.

Eating pasta or other foods high in carbohydrates the night before the race is always a good idea. The most important thing to do during the last few meals is to make sure you eat food that your body is use to digesting. Get in a good meal the night before, since you will be eating only a light breakfast the next morning, but don't overdo it. Of course, drink plenty of water during the forty-eight hours prior to the big run.

Back to Example 3: The More Advanced Marathoner

For the more experienced, advanced runner, these recommendations should be used in accordance with what you are already comfortable with. The fact that you are attempting to run the marathon in three hours (3:20 for women), means you must be doing something right. The twelve week training program suggested on page 98 can be considered as offering general directions rather than a guide to be followed point by point. You may be able to accomplish your goal by running less mileage each week, or you may want to run more. There are a few aspects to my suggested plan that you may find useful to incorporate into your training schedule.

12 Weeks Training is Enough

First, setting aside 12 weeks to train for the race is plenty of time. You ought to be in good shape just from your routine training. You are able to accomplish more in your training, in terms of quality and quantity, in the same amount of time as someone else attempting to run the marathon in the 3:30 to 4:00 hour range. Do not make the mistake of overtraining, and thereby leaving your best runs out there in the far reaches of your neighborhood, instead of at the race.

Speed Workouts

Second, I recommend you spend at least a few weeks during the middle of your training doing speed workouts on a track. Commonly referred to as interval training, these workouts serve to increase your leg muscle strength, as well as improve your running style and mental toughness. For specific workout suggestions, please refer to the section on speed workouts for marathon training in Chapter 7, *Speed Training*.

In order to make a smooth transition to doing speed workouts, especially for those runners with limited experience on a track, start out once a week for the first few weeks with a **quick tempo run**. Essentially, the idea behind the quick tempo run is to set aside specific periods of the run to surge for a limited time. For example, after using the first mile-and-a-half as a warmup, begin surging for three minutes, and then return to your usual pace for six minutes. Repeat the exercise four more times, for a total of five surges. End the run with a mile-and-a-half warm-down.

Two 20-Plus Milers

Do two long runs of 20 miles or more. The last one should occur no later than three weeks before the marathon. In order to maximize the quality of the second run, I suggest giving yourself two weeks time in between the two runs. For instance, do the first 20 miler in week seven, and the second in week nine.

In week eight, don't go beyond 15-16 miles on your long run, so that your legs get a bit of a break before the final 20-plus mile run. Some runners at this level are inclined to do more than two 20 mile runs. Don't go beyond three 20 milers. The timing of when you do them is more important than how many you run.

It's not going to help, from an endurance perspective, to run a 20 miler less than two weeks prior to the race. It may even hurt you. You could end up at the starting line with tired legs. For the same reason, avoid running a 20 miler too early in your training before you have gone through the proper build-up stage.

TABLE 10: 12 WEEK, THREE HOUR MARATHON TRAINING SCHEDULE						
M	**T**	**W**	**Th**	**F**	**S**	**Su**
Week 1 8	10	6	srg	6	12	6
Week 2 8	11	6	srg	6	13-14	6
Week 3 8	11	6	speed	6	15	6
Week 4 8	12-13	6	speed	6	16-17	6
Week 5 8	12-13	6	speed	7-8	18	6
Week 6 8	12-13	6	speed	7-8	18	6
Week 7 8	12-13	6	speed	7-8	20	6
Week 8 8	12-13	6	speed	7-8	15	6
Week 9 8	12	6	speed	7	20-22	6
Week 10 8	10	6	speed	6	16-17	6
Week 11 8	6	srg	6	13	4-5	off
Week 12 6	3-4	srg*	off	4-5	2-3	race

Srg = surge
*abbreviated workout: 3 3 mins. surges, 4 mins. recovery

Tapering Off Is Still Important

Finally, allow yourself enough time towards the end of your training to rest up for the big race. I suggest using the last three weeks as a tapering off period in which your weekly mileage should decline significantly. All those months of intense training will not wither away as result of reducing the mileage leading up to the race.

I'm not suggesting that you make all your runs short and easy during the last three weeks. Do a solid 16-17 mile run in the first week of tapering. You still need to keep your legs accustomed to the longer distances. In the following week, shorten the run to about 12 or 13 miles. That run, around ten days before the race, should be the last run of any significant distance. Overall, your weekly mileage ought to be cut by more than half from the peak of three weeks ago.

MARATHON DAY

Marathon day has finally arrived. The months of laborious training are over. Now comes the fun part. Your body, which you have honed into a fine-tuned running machine, is wound up and ready to go. You should be overwhelmed by a tremendous feeling of accomplishment, excitement, and most of all, confidence at the starting line as you wait for the race to begin.

Pre-Race Preparation

Let's start with breakfast. Get up early enough so that you can eat something at least three hours before the race. Don't eat too much, but try to get something substantial down. Avoid all dairy and meat products. Bacon and eggs with a glass of milk or orange juice is definitely out. Also avoid citrus fruits. They are far too acidic for marathon day. Anything with a lot of sugar takes too much energy to digest.

What can be included in the boring race day diet? Stick to water as your choice of liquid. A couple of fluffy pancakes without syrup or butter is my favorite pre-race meal. A bagel without cream cheese or butter is not a bad idea. The one fruit of choice is definitely the banana. Bananas are the easiest fruit to digest. Oatmeal made with water is fine, and so are all the bran cereals as long as you use water, or a very limited amount of skim milk.

It's a good idea to do some stretching before the start of the race, but you don't need to do a warm-up run. A short walk should be all you need to loosen yourself up a bit before stretching. Use the first mile or so of the marathon as your warm-up run, since you will likely be forced to be run slower than your planned pace at the beginning due to the large crowd of runners bunched together at the start. Also, stay in the shade and off your feet before and after your stretch when you are waiting around for the race to start.

Running the Race
The two most important things to be concerned about during the race are water and pace. Let's start first with pace.

Run At Your Own Pace
Prior to the marathon, you will have determined what pace per mile to shoot for. That pace will be in your head during the entire race. Unless, you are really good with numbers, you may want to write down on your arm what your **splits** should be every mile, or two to three miles. *A split is the time that has elapsed as you reach particular distances of the race.* If for example, you are shooting for an eight minute per mile pace, your split at three miles is twenty-four minutes.

You will be tempted early in the race to run under the pace you are hoping to maintain for the entire marathon. Be careful about not starting out too fast. It will almost surely come back to haunt you later in the race. For instance, if your goal is to maintain an 8:30 pace, do not start out running eight minute miles.

The exception to this rule is if you were forced to run the first mile or two well below your anticipated pace because of the crowded field at the start. If you were forced to run the first mile in ten minutes, then it's okay to run the second in eight minutes. Do not, however, attempt to make up the entire lost time by maintaining that faster pace for more than one mile. And don't attempt to go much beyond the 30 seconds below your planned pace in order to make up the time quickly. The best advice is to simply deduct the lost time from the first mile from your final time.

This does not mean there is no point during the marathon where, if able, you can run faster than your forecasted pace. The first half of the marathon, however, is not the time to try it. Wait until you have gone over twenty miles.

In the case of the marathon, the second half of the race does not begin at thirteen miles. It starts at twenty. The last six miles are likely to be as demanding as the entire first twenty to complete. This is where all those "hitting the wall" stories your fellow marathoners talk about take place. We'll discuss this in more detail shortly.

If you are still feeling strong as you pass the 21st-mile mark (there should be **mile marks** posted at every mile of the race), then consider increasing your pace a bit. Still, don't go for broke. Try knocking 15-30 seconds or so off your pace for the next few miles. It's quite an achievement to be able to finish the last six miles of the marathon at a faster pace than the first 20. (Unless, of course, you run the first 20 far below your potential.)

The Importance of Water

I cannot stress enough how important it is to drink water throughout the race. I learned the hard way. In my first marathon I made the mistake of waiting until I felt thirsty to start drinking water. I put off stopping for water until well into the second half of the race. Even then, I did not drink enough at first, because I was too concerned about wasting time. My impatient behavior came back to haunt me at the end. During the last four miles of the race, I was in a state of near-dehydration. My pace slowed dramatically, from about five and a half minutes per mile to over eight. Basically, my body decided to shut down, just like an overheated engine.

The truth is, you end up saving precious minutes by taking the time to stop often for water. Most marathons have water stations about every two and a half miles on the course. It's important early on, even when your body shows no signs of being thirsty, to stop and take a drink. Stop briefly at each and drink about a half cup of water. It's far better to take small amounts of water often throughout the race than to start gulping down huge quantities towards the middle or the end.

Some people are able to pick up a cup of water and drink it almost without breaking stride. It's a great trick, but not easy to do. For most of us, attempting to maintain your pace while also trying to grab and drink a cup of water results in a fair amount of spilling and even some spitting up. Unless you are extremely slight of hand and have a sturdy stomach, just slow down to a walk while picking up the cup and drinking it. The entire process takes less than ten seconds. Trust me, taking that brief time to do it right will save you time over the entire 26 miles.

There are usually a couple of high energy sports drinks, such as Gatorade, that are available at the water stations. Stick to water, unless you are accustomed to drinking these sports beverages while you run and not just afterwards. Because most of the flavoring in these drinks is citrus-based, they tend to burn the stomach a bit when taken while running. It has happened to me, even though I'm conditioned to drinking tons of the stuff after I run.

These drinks are also frequently on hand at shorter races, such as 10-Ks. You can use these races to try them out, but remember, you cannot lose sticking with water. Shorter races also offer you the opportunity to get your drinking stops down to an art form. It's not as rudimentary a process as you might think.

Hitting the Wall

There is one aspect of the race that marathoners of all levels fear. It's commonly referred to as **hitting the wall**. This is the point in the marathon, usually between the 20 mile mark and the end, when your body decides to begin cutting off power.

It's not like blowing a couple of tires at high speed and then suddenly coming to a screeching halt. It's more like a feeling of nausea experienced on a rolling boat by someone who has yet to develop sea legs and which, over a brief period of time, becomes progressively worse. If it happens, don't panic. Hitting the wall usually doesn't produce violent stomach upheavals.

The good news is that hitting the wall is an experience faced by only a fraction of the participants in a marathon. The chances of it occurring to someone who trains properly and runs a smart race is small. For almost every runner, the last six miles are the toughest. It's likely your pace over this period will slow somewhat, but not dramatically. Try not to panic, as you begin to tire towards the end of the race. This can cause you to believe that you are worse off than you actually are. Don't make the mistake of talking yourself into hitting the wall. It's only natural to feel exhausted over the last few miles, but try not to let it defeat you mentally.

One way to help prevent hitting the wall is to have done proper weight training in the months prior to the marathon. Refer to Chapter 11, *Cross Training*, for more details. Your increased upper body strength, developed by lifting weights, helps to compensate for the lack of strength remaining in your legs, as well as the light feeling in your head. Your arms, chest, and shoulders work harder while the rest of your body goes on automatic pilot.

The most important tool to rely on if you hit the wall is your mind. As bad as you may feel, keep reminding yourself that it will all be over soon. If it really gets rough, walk for a short period, but try to maintain a brisk pace. Keep your mind focused on how far you have already gone, and remind yourself how little remains in comparison. Finally, let the crowds inspire you to continue on.

Crossing the Finish Line

The consequences of hitting the wall should not be the note on which to end this chapter. Regardless of your condition at the end of the marathon, there is no greater feeling than crossing that finish line. Most runners feel an extraordinary sense of accomplishment. Others just feel relieved. There are always some in the race who are disappointed with their performance. But they all share the special camaraderie of becoming a marathoner.

---

5 THINGS TO REMEMBER ON MARATHON RACE DAY

1. *Don't overeat on the morning of the race.*
2. *Stop often to drink water during the race.*
3. *Don't start off too fast.*
4. *Wait until after 20 miles to make a move.*
5. *Remain tough mentally once you begin to tire physically.*

7. SPEED TRAINING

Simply put, **speed training** is tough. During my college days, my heart was beating as fast before the start of an interval workout on Wednesday as it was moments before the start of a race on Saturday. In a sense, a speed workout demands more from you than a race. The adrenaline is always flowing during a race. It's not as easy to get yourself motivated to give it your all for a weekday speed workout.

A speed workout can be loosely defined as any training session in which you run at a significantly faster pace than your usual training pace. It's not for everyone. Those who run for the sheer enjoyment of the sport, or to stay in shape, don't need to take the plunge. If, however, you fall into the category of runners who are driven by the need to improve their times, there are several reasons why you should subject yourself to the rigors of speed training.

WHY DO SPEED WORKOUTS?

First, speed workouts are important because **they simulate race conditions**. Training at a pace equal to or even faster than the speed you run a race helps to prepare you physically and mentally for competition. You're guaranteed to go into any 10-K race or marathon more mentally tough and physically equipped after incorporating speed workouts as a routine part of your training.

More specifically, speed workouts **increase your muscle strength** and transform your entire body into a more physiologically efficient machine. As you start to run faster your body begins to lose its ability to replace oxygen as quickly as it used to. This causes waste products such as lactic acid to accumulate in your muscles. As you become fitter, your body becomes more efficient in replacing the oxygen used by your muscles. This allows you to run faster for longer periods of time without accumulating significant amounts of unfriendly byproducts in your muscles.

Enough with the science lesson. Speed workouts also serve to **improve your concentration and running style**. Your arm movement and posture tend to improve when you are focusing on picking up the pace. Finally, speed training adds **variety** to your running schedule.

Much of the information in the next few sections has already been covered in earlier chapters, but I've summarized it for you here for easy reference.

Interval Training and Ladder Workouts

The most common type of speed workout, usually referred to as **interval training**, is most often performed on a track. A typical workout consists of running repeated distances ranging from 200 meters to 1 mile. The shorter distances (200-400 meters) are run at an almost all-out effort. The longer intervals (800 meters to 1 mile) are run at a more controlled speed.

Speed workouts for those training for a marathon will concentrate more on the longer distances, while the 10-K enthusiasts should target the shorter and intermediate distances. A workout can either consist of repeats of one specific distance, or combine varying distances in an up and down progression, commonly referred to as a **ladder workout**.

Although a track is the most obvious place to run a speed workout, I recommend that you occasionally seek out a softer, more shock-absorbing surface, such as grass or dirt. It's especially important if your focus will be on doing the longer interval distances.

Surge Training

Another form of somewhat less intense speed training is known as **surge** or **quick tempo running**. The purpose of these runs is to accelerate your pace for a given period of time (usually between 1 to 3 minutes) and then return to your original training pace. The process is repeated until you have completed 4 to 6 surges.

The time of acceleration and "rest" can be planned prior to a surge run or improvised as you go along. Improvisation works well in a group running session. Each runner can take a turn leading the charge and calling out the length of time the surge or acceleration will be maintained. More details and specific training suggestions on surge running appear in the intermediate sections of Chapters 5 and 6.

Adding speed workouts to your schedule is done in the same gradual manner as the endurance component of your training. The following are some suggested workouts for intermediate and advanced runners training for 10-Ks and marathons. Consider these recommendations more as a general framework from which to create your own routine. Don't feel constrained by the need to comply with every aspect of the following workout suggestions.

SPEED WORKOUTS FOR 10-K TRAINING
Intermediate Level

It's not essential for intermediate level 10-K runners to do speed workouts. In most cases, a surge run once a week will provide you with enough of a change in pace. But for those who want to give interval training a chance, I have provided an eight week workout guide. Use the first and last two weeks of a 12 week 10-K training program for surge runs once a week. The speed workouts suggested here would begin in the third week of in-season training and would end during the 10th week.

At a minimum, run an easy mile-and-a-half to two miles warm-up before starting the speed workout. Your warm-down afterwards should be at least two miles. During the workout, be conscious about not allowing yourself too much rest time between intervals. The next table provides recommended recovery periods. The speed at which you run the intervals should be below your targeted race pace, especially for the shorter ones. Shoot for consistency. Try to do the last quarter or half mile repeat as fast as the first.

TABLE 11: 10-K SPEED WORKOUTS - INTERMEDIATE LEVEL

Week 1	4x400 meters, 90 second recovery between
Week 2	200-400-600-400-200, 90 second recovery
Week 3	6x400, 2 sets of 3, 90 sec. recovery, 1/4 jog between sets
Week 4	200-600-800-600-200, 90 second recovery
Week 5	3x800, 2 minute recovery between
Week 6	400-600-800-600-400, 90 second recovery
Week 7	5x400, 90 second recovery
Week 8	200-400-600-400-200, 90 second recovery

Advanced Level

Speed workouts are almost a must for an advanced runner hoping to improve his 10-K performance. As described in the 10-K chapter, *I loosely define **advanced** as any man or woman capable of breaking 40 and 45 minutes, respectively.* Table 12 (on the next page) contains a 12 week speed training schedule to coincide with the 12 week in-season 10-K training schedule appearing in the 10-K chapter.

The schedule begins with a modest level of speed training (1.5 to 1.75 miles) in order to give you time to make the adjustment of adding intervals to your training routine. The middle weeks are when the workouts are the longest (2 to 2.5 miles). The last few weeks the intervals taper off (1.5 to 1 mile) to keep your legs fresh for your final couple of 10-K races of the season.

Run about two easy miles before starting each speed workout. Get in at least a 2-3 mile warm-down after the interval session.

TABLE 12: 10-K SPEED WORKOUT SCHEDULE - ADVANCED LEVEL

Week 1	6x400 meters, 60 second recovery between
Week 2	3x800, 90 second recovery
Week 3	400-600-800-600-400, 60 second recovery between, 90 seconds after 800 interval
Week 4	8x400, 2 sets of 4, 60 second recovery, 1/4 mile jog between sets
Week 5	4x800, 90 second recovery
Week 6	400-600-800-800-600-400, 60 second recovery, 1/4 mile jog between 800s
Week 7	10x400, 2 sets of 5, 60 second recovery, 1/4 mile jog between sets
Week 8	5x800, 90 second recovery, 1/4 mile jog between 2nd and 3rd 800
Week 9	200-400-600-800-600-400-200, 60 second recovery, 1/4 mile jog after 800
Week 10	6x 400, 60 second recovery
Week 11	200-400-600-600-400-200, 60 second recovery, 1/4 mile jog between 600s
Week 12	4x400, 60 second recovery

Try to stick to the recovery periods between each interval recommended in the table. There's no point in concentrating on improving your speed at the expense of not also working on endurance. Sticking close to these recovery times will ensure that these workouts benefit both your speed and endurance capabilities. As always, strive for consistency. With some effort, that last 800 meter repeat will not be more than a few seconds slower than the first.

SPEED WORKOUTS FOR MARATHON TRAINING

Only advanced marathon runners make speed workouts part of their weekly marathon training routine. *As mentioned in the marathon chapter, I roughly defined advanced as those women and men who target running times at or below 3:20 and 3:00 respectively.* The following speed training schedule contains eight weeks of workouts. It's designed to coincide with the middle eight weeks of the 12 week marathon training schedule appearing in the advanced section of the marathon chapter.

TABLE 13: MARATHON SPEED WORKOUTS

Week 1	8x400 meters, 2 sets of 4, 60 second recovery between intervals, 1/4 mile jog between sets
Week 2	4x800, 90 second recovery
Week 3	400-800-1200-800-400, 90 second recovery, 1/4 mile jog after 1200
Week 4	3x1 mile, 1/4 mile jog recovery
Week 5*	3x800, 90 second recovery
Week 6	800-1200-1600-1200, 90 second recovery, 1/4 mile jog after 1600
Week 7*	6x400, 2 sets of 3, 60 second recovery, 1/4 mile jog between sets
Week 8	400-400-800-800-400-400, 60 second recovery, 1/4 mile jog between 800s

*weeks containing a long run of 20 or more miles - interval workout reduced.

Always get in a good warm-up and warm-down before and after doing a speed workout. It really helps to have at least one other person to run the sessions with, especially on the days of the longer interval distances.

Generally, the workouts start somewhat modest (a total of 2 miles), rise in distance during the middle weeks (2.5 to 3 miles), and taper off towards the end. Weeks five and seven are purposely scheduled to be light. These are the two workouts meant to correspond with the weeks you plan to run 20 or more miles on your long day. It's a good idea to ease up a bit on speed workouts leading up to important long runs.

8. ISSUES FOR WOMEN

SAFETY
In the United States today, every 17 seconds someone becomes a victim of a violent crime. Every minute, 1.3 rapes of adult women occur. Crimes against women are rising at a significantly faster rate than total crime: during the past ten years, rape rates have risen nearly three times as fast as the total crime rate.

There are no national statistics on how many women have been assaulted while running. But many of us know of at least one friend who has been threatened or assaulted during a run. Just recently, I read about a woman who was raped while running on the popular Central Park reservoir loop in New York City.

Precautions
Women running today always have to be careful, no matter when or where they choose to run. There are many precautions women can take to reduce the risks of assault while running. Martt Langelan, an experienced self-defense instructor and past president of the Washington, D.C. Rape Crisis Center, has given me her recommendations, based on research of what actually happens in attempted rapes and other assaults:

1. Vary Your Running Routes
Don't set up a predictable pattern of running. Always running along the same path at the same time makes it too easy for someone to learn your routine and jump you.

2. Don't Run Anywhere You Would Not Feel Safe Walking

A surprise attack can overcome the swiftest runner. Run in well-populated areas, and save your invincible attitude for the unfriendly dogs, inclement weather, and weekend 10-Ks.

3. Know Your Routes

Pay attention to safe places along the way. *Safety = people + lights.* As you run each day this week, look around you at three minute intervals: decide which way you'd run for help if you needed it along each section of your path. Notice who would be around to hear you if you yelled for help at the times of day you're out there. Think about your options **now**, so you'll be prepared to react fast if you do need to get to safety.

In daylight, with a friend or two, check out potential traps. Is that alley a dead end? What's behind the hedge? Are there places along your routes where someone could hide easily? If you regularly run past blind spots — alleys, large trees, bushes, boulders, or sharp corners that block your vision — swing wide as you go by those points, to minimize the chance that anyone could grab you.

4. Run With a Friend

There is safety in numbers. Many running clubs organize daily and weekend group runs. Clubs also offer a way to meet other runners who will be happy to join you on your own runs.

5. If You Have a Dog, Take Fido Along

While other humans are usually your best protection, running with a large dog will also make you look less vulnerable. But a dog that is too small or too undisciplined to keep up with you is not much of a deterrent.

6. Run During Daylight Hours and Vary Your Times

Even during the daytime, it's smart to vary the time of day when you run as a way of further reducing your predictability. Start out fifteen minutes earlier one day, fifteen minutes later the next. If you absolutely must run after dark, do it **only** with a friend or two, and vary both your routes and your times. A solo night run is a high-risk proposition for anyone, male or female — don't do it!

7. Leave the Walkmans at Home

Wearing headphones makes it impossible for you to hear an attacker approaching, and makes you look like a much-too-easy target for assault. Your eyes and ears are your early warning system — use them!

Pay attention to your surroundings. A few extra seconds of response time can make an enormous difference in your safety. As you run, take a second to really look at the people you pass. In self-defense classes, women learn to do the "observation circle" as a matter of habit: train yourself to notice at least three details about anyone moving within a 20-foot radius of you — clothes, glasses, haircut, height — anything that could help you to identify them later if you had to.

8. Be Smart About Handling People Who Try to Stop You or Harass You

Stay in motion. Stopping makes you an easier target. If people ask you for directions, wave and keep on going; don't risk your safety just to be nice. They can find someone else to ask.

Never stop when harassers yell at you on the street or in the park. Some men feel threatened by athletic women and take their aggression out on women who run. A stranger's explicit comments about your body are no compliment, and many harassers' crude, ugly comments are downright threatening.

Don't yell back obscenities, but don't ignore harassment either. Shout, "**Stop harassing women!**" without breaking stride. Many women who are now using that response say that it's very effective. That short, sharp statement has some real content, and often shocks the harasser into silence.

9. Carry a Weapon You Can Use

A whistle or siren alarm may not bring help. You're better off relying on your own resources: your alertness, speed, and mental preparation. Mace and pepper gas are useless if they're in your pocket instead of in your hand; if you carry one of these, have it out, uncapped and ready to use, and get some practice aiming it beforehand. (If the wind is blowing the wrong way, you can miss entirely, or gas yourself.)

One of the best weapons is a simple set of keys. Carry them with the points together, in your closed fist, and use the keys as a jabbing, stabbing implement against the attacker. (Don't spread the keys between your fingers – you'll injure your own hand if you strike someone that way.) Any sharp object – keys, a ballpoint pen, or even a stick – can be used as a weapon to stab an attacker's eyes, throat, or groin.

Other General Safety Tips

There is no specific profile for a "bad guy." You should even be suspicious of other runners. Anyone can dress like a runner; keep your guard up. If you think another runner is following you, don't hesitate to deviate from your normal course and head for the nearest safe place. Pay attention to your gut-level radar – picking up on something in his body language or behavior that's making you uncomfortable. Trust your intuition. If your situation feels creepy, it *is* creepy – and potentially dangerous. Get to safety.

One of the best preventive measures is a short self-defense class at your local YWCA or rape crisis center – you'll be mentally prepared to react fast, and you'll learn some simple techniques that really work. In a basic self-defense course you'll learn how to break free from a front or back choke, an arm choke, and other grabs. You don't need to be incredibly strong to get loose, but you do need to know what works, the kinds of tactics that will get you out of various holds. They are not hard to learn, and they may save your life.

Some tactics rarely succeed. Crying, begging, pleading with an assailant, telling him you're pregnant, or saying you have AIDS or VD – all of those play right into the attacker's power trip, and none have a very high success rate in actually stopping an attack.

What To Do if You are Attacked

There are strategies that do work in many cases. If you are attacked, Langelan recommends the following steps:

1.Resist Immediately

The first few minutes of an attack are the best "window of opportunity" to escape. In attempted rapes, women who fight back right away are not only less likely to be raped, but also less likely to be otherwise injured than women who do not resist. If someone grabs you, react as quickly as possible.

2. Yell and Keep on Yelling

If the attacker is unarmed, your voice is your first line of defense. Don't shout "Help!" or "Fire!" or "Rape!" — that doesn't work. Shout "No!" or a karate yell like "Ki-Ya!" right in the assailant's face. Sometimes, that sharp yell alone is enough to startle him and make him let go of you. Take off fast, as soon as he loosens his hold.

If he's still coming after you, start telling anyone around you what's going on and what to do: Yell at the top of your lungs, "This is an attack! Call the cops!" That yell works to get bystanders into action. It turns out that people are much more likely to help if you tell them what you want them to do.

3. Use a Combination of Tactics to Break Loose

If the first tactic doesn't work, try another. Keep fighting. Most assailants are looking for victims they can overpower easily. Women who use a combination of physical self-defense tactics significantly increase their chances of stopping the attack.

Your legs are the strongest part of your body — start kicking! Think and aim. Direct your kicks at the attacker's knees and ankles, and kick hard. (A knee to the groin is less effective, and trying a high kick to the groin may make you fall.)

- If he's behind you, reach back, grab his genitals, and twist. Stomp on the arch of his foot with all your weight. Swing your elbow back hard into his solar plexus.

- If his hands are on your throat, arms, or legs, grab one of his fingers and yank it backward hard and fast, to peel the hand off your body.

- If you have keys in your hand, jab them into his eyes, his throat, or his groin.

- If you get knocked to the ground, kick hard at his face and temples. And keep yelling as you do it!

- If he's dragging you towards a vehicle, fight for all you're worth. You are much more likely to survive if you fight where the incident starts, than if you get taken to an isolated location.

As soon as you break loose, run for the nearest safe place along your route. Keep yelling until you get to safety.

Most rapists are unarmed. If, however, the attacker has a weapon, your first priority is to get the weapon away from your body. It can be risky to yell at someone who has a knife or gun right on you; try a strong negotiating tactic, to get the weapon down. Use a "broken record" technique — keep talking, and give specific instructions: "Put the knife in your pocket. I don't like knives, I've never liked them. You don't need that here, you can put it away right now. Just put it back in your pocket . . . ." As soon as the weapon is away from your body, break loose, start yelling, and sprint for safety.

Runners are unlikely targets for robberies (after all, we're not carrying much worth stealing when we're out on a run). But if someone does demand money, give it to them. Move slow and easy, keep your hands in sight, put your loose money, wallet, or pack on the ground, and say, "Here you go, no problem," and start backing away. This is no time for heroics. Your wallet can be replaced —you can't be. The mugger will go after your wallet while you back up, and once you're 10 or 12 feet from the attacker, he's not likely to kill you even if he does take a shot at you (most street muggers are lousy marksmen).

These and many other successful techniques for dealing with harassers, rapists, and muggers are detailed in Langelan's new book, *Back Off! How to Confront and Stop Sexual Harassment and Harassers* (Simon & Schuster, 1993). *Back Off!* is lively reading, with dozens of success stories from men, women, and children (including runners and cyclists who succeeded in stopping all kinds of assailants.

I hope you never have to deal with the experience of trying to repel an attacker. One of the best aspects of running is being able to have some time to yourself to escape completely from all the complications posed by the outside world. It's regrettable that in today's world, women can't have this luxury while running.

RUNNING BEFORE & AFTER PREGNANCY

All women who become pregnant should be examined on a regular basis by a physician and receive their approval for continuing with any sort of strenuous athletic activities, including running. Any pregnant woman who falls into the category of **high risk** probably should not run at all during their pregnancy, even if they are in excellent running shape. Running during pregnancy is also not advised for those who have not done much running in the past. It's never a good idea to start a new routine of exercise once you become pregnant.

In the case of experienced runners not at high risk, continuing to run during pregnancy does not endanger the health of your baby or yourself. Most physicians believe it's okay to run during the first trimester, when the fetus is at its most vulnerable period of development. If something is going to happen in this period to someone not considered to be in the high risk category, it will happen whether you are running or not. But ask your doctor specifically about this topic; there are some in the medical community who advise against running during the first trimester.

There are some basic danger signs that pregnant women should be conscious of while running. If you experience bleeding or sharp pains, stop immediately and get in contact with your doctor. You also never want to be out of breath while running. You should always be able to talk without losing your breath. Try not to allow your heart rate to go beyond 140 to 160 beats-per-minute.

Running close to your normal distance is fine, but slow down your pace a bit. At the end of your run, walk for a while as a cool down.

WHAT TO WEAR!

It's a good idea to wear two running bras. Another good suggestion is to purchase a one-piece spandex or lycra workout outfit a size or two larger than what you normally wear.

Most women are able to run through the first six months of pregnancy. After six months, your physical situation starts to hamper your ability to run. Swimming towards the end of your pregnancy offers a good alternative to running. It's refreshing, and more importantly, a weightless form of exercise you can do three or four days a week for 15-30 minutes. During the last week of your pregnancy, or if you are overdo, walking is probably the most advisable form of exercise.

Post-Partum Issues

Following your pregnancy, don't start running again until after your six week check-up. A good point of return is eight weeks after post-partum. Take it slow at first. Ease back into your training. Don't worry if you feel overly tired as you start to run again. As prior to giving birth, it's a good idea to continue to wear two running bras. If you are breast feeding, try to run after nursing when your breasts are empty. It will probably take about four months until you feel you are back to normal.

After pregnancy, many women experience bladder control problems, especially while they run. There are exercises you can do before and after pregnancy that strengthen your pelvic muscles. Called **Kegel** exercises after Dr. Arnold Kegel, the gynecologist who popularized them, the exercises help to limit the probability of experiencing bladder control problems. Squeeze and release the muscle responsible for stopping the flow of urine midstream while urinating. This serves to strengthen the pelvic-floor muscles.

A typical exercise routine recommended by Dr. Kristene Whitmore, Director of the Incontinence Center at Graduate Hospital in Philadelphia, can start with three sets of three contractions; hold each for three seconds, and then relax for three seconds. Work up to three sets of ten contractions, each held for ten seconds at a time, for a total of 60-90 contractions a day.

Running with a Baby Jogger

Many mothers like to put their newest addition to the family into a **baby jogger** and bring the baby along on their run. Dads can do it too. The baby should be at least six months old. It's important to wait until your baby is able to lift his or her head up. Be sure to check with your pediatrician first. Also, don't expose the baby to the sun! Make sure they wear a hat and are protected by sun screen. The sun can burn right through their sensitive skin, which is not used to being exposed to sunlight.

It's a good idea to avoid running with the baby in the middle of the day. Try to run in the morning or late afternoon. Avoid extreme heat or cold. Remember, running can warm you up pretty easily, but the baby doesn't get any warmer from just sitting in the jogger.

If you run with a baby jogger, be sure to use extra caution at intersections. Due to the length of the jogger, the front wheel sticks out far beyond where you actually stop when approaching an intersection. Because of this, try to get used to stopping far in advanced of what you are accustomed to. Once at the intersection, it's a good idea to turn the jogger backwards in order to keep the front wheel from sticking out into traffic.

Running with a baby jogger adds to your workout. Your arms and shoulders will surely benefit from the combination of pushing the jogger and your baby. The jogger itself is actually quite light. The newest models weigh as little as six pounds. But when you add the weight of your baby, you're talking about pushing an extra 30 pounds or so. Don't expect to be able to follow your routine running schedule when using the baby jogger. You are likely to find yourself running longer and slower, and having to stop during the run to keep a check on the baby. If both of you are game, you can keep running with your child in the jogger until he or she reaches the age of four.

AMENORRHEA: AN ISSUE FOR WOMEN RUNNERS!

Amenorrhea, the lack of experiencing a normal menstrual cycle over a prolonged period, affects three percent of women of child-bearing age at any given time in the U.S. A universal time standard, in terms of the number of months of not experiencing menstrual bleeding, does not exist for determining the presence of amenorrhea. Recent medical studies have used time durations ranging form three months to a year. Most doctors will diagnose a woman with amenorrhea if they have not been menstruating for three to six months.

The medical community is not completely sure why amenorrhea is more prevalent among athletes. A combination of too much exercise and too little calorie intake appears to be the most common cause of amenorrhea among athletes. Other factors besides diet and heightened physical activity that may cause amenorrhea include: genetic background, increased stress, and reproductive experiences.

Why should women be concerned about amenorrhea? The lack of normal menstrual cycles may cause women to develop **osteoporosis**. Osteoporosis refers to premature bone loss or inadequate bone formation resulting in low bone mass, or "weak bones." Twenty million women suffer from osteoporosis. Women are five times more likely than men to suffer from the disease. People diagnosed with osteoporosis become more susceptible to hip, spine, wrist, and leg fractures.

The lack of normal menstrual cycles usually reduces women's **estrogen** levels. Estrogen is a key ingredient for maintaining proper bone health. A number of other factors also influence bone health including genetics, nutrition, body fat, and emotional and pyhsical stress.

In the case of women runners, especially those following demand-ing training schedules, studies have shown a strong link between amenorrhea and symptoms connected to osteoporosis. Bone loss in an amenorrheic athlete is rapid and may not be completely reversible.

If you have not had normal menstrual cycles over a number of months, consult a doctor to find out what is causing your condition. Modifications in your diet and training routine may, in some cases, result in your normal menstrual cycle returning.

A common fallacy associated with amenorrhea is that it can cause women to experience child bearing problems in the future. Studies have shown no connection between amenorrhea and complications associated with pregnancy.

9. MENTAL TOUGHNESS

Yogi Berra once said, "50 percent of baseball is 80 percent mental."
Woody Allen is famous for saying, "90 percent of life is just showing
up." Both Woody and Yogi are on the right track. Whether in life,
baseball or running, having a strong mental attitude is vital to
success.

There are two major components to developing a mentally tough
approach towards running. The first and most important quality is
discipline. The other major factor is having the capacity to remain
relaxed when you feel pushed to your limit physically.

DISCIPLINE
Success in running depends to a large extent on being disciplined.
You are ahead of the game just by showing a willingness to stick to
a consistent running schedule that is in line with your abilities.
Whether you are able to meet the specific training goals you have
set for yourself at a particular time is not as important as remaining
committed to making the effort. Falling a minute short of the time
you set out to achieve for the spring 10-K season does not
necessarily mean you have failed mentally.

The inability to meet your goal should be attributed to your mental
state only if, for instance, over the course of the winter, you decided
to deviate from your normal training by taking two weeks off due
to slightly inclement weather. Similarly, setting out to do seven
miles on a particular day and deciding while you run to cut it down
to four because you are recovering from a stubborn cold is alright.

It is not okay, however, to shorten the run merely because you are feeling lazy or sense a touch of fatigue coming over you.

STAYING RELAXED

Probably the toughest mental hurdle to get over is remaining relaxed when under physical duress. On one of those more trying days you have to tell yourself, "I'm not feeling so great or enjoying this that much right now, but I can get through it. In another few miles I'll be done and feel a lot better about being able to complete today's run." It's about being able to compensate for physical discomfort with a strong mental outlook, instead of allowing your physical condition to dictate how you feel mentally.

It's better to focus on the pain when it hits you on a run than trying to ignore or fight it. I call it internalizing the pain. Too many runners turn a minor inconvenience, like a sudden cramp or feeling of fatigue towards the end of a run, into a major dilemma because they let their mind blow it out of proportion. Think more deeply about this sudden problem. Upon greater reflection, you are likely to realize it's not so bad after all.

I'm always telling my running friends that one of the most important factors for gauging success is how well you are able to get through those days when you are feeling less than 100 percent. That's more important than how well you are able to get through the tough workouts on days when you feel great. Getting through those down days more than anything else keeps you on schedule towards achieving your goal.

The more you are able to remain relaxed, the easier it is to run harder. During track and cross country races in college and the 10-Ks I've run more recently, it always hurt the least on the days when I ran my best times. On those days I was able to reach a higher level of concentration. The motto for running is not, "No pain, no gain." It's more like, "Run past the pain, and you will gain."

During one of my better cross country races in college, I was so focused on keeping up with the other team's top runner, whose past times topped anything I had ever done, that I almost fell into a trance. My eyes remained completely focused on the back of his racing top. My ears shielded out noises except for those being made by my opponent, so that I could concentrate on remaining in sync with his breathing and steps. I was too engaged in the race to worry about being tired. I did not win the race, but I did finish within ten seconds of him and ran my best time for the season. I felt good throughout the race and ran a fast time.

In one of my worst performances on the track during my senior year in college, it was a totally different story. I was running a 5000 meter race, and by midway, I was unable to keep pace with the lead pack of runners. I began to let my mind wander away from the race. I picked up on all the small talk going on in the infield of the track. I started to take an interest in the spectators sitting in the stands. More than anything else, I began to focus on how lousy I felt and I just wanted the race to be over. I felt terrible and ran a time far slower than what I was capable of.

Being mentally tough is not something you can achieve by simply embracing a theory. Sitting around before a run and thinking about staying tough does not work. You must practice it. It's not something that can be learned in terms of remaining true to an idea, such as thinking positively about it. You cannot dictate when you want to use it. It has to kick in during the most uncomfortable moments when your mind is receiving conflicting signals from the rest of your body.

In running, it's the power to remain calm when pressed physically that separates those who get the most out of their abilities from the underachievers. It's not easy to accomplish, but well worth it when you cross the finish line and achieve your goal.

10. INJURIES & HOW TO AVOID THEM

Unfortunately, for a large number of runners at all levels of ability, injuries are too common an occurrence. Don't let them get the best of you. Try to accept the fact that injuries are an almost unavoidable part of the running experience.

With some luck, most of you will only suffer minor injuries over the course of your running careers. The damage does not have to be serious or pose a significant threat to your training routine if you're willing to show a combination of restraint and determination during your recovery period.

I suffered two injuries during my college cross-country days. The more serious one occurred in a race during the summer before my junior year when I tore my left calf muscle. I was completely out of action for six weeks. I spent about eight weeks doing rehabilitation exercises on a Cybex machine. I missed the entire first part of the cross country season, and was not able to run at 100 percent for the rest of the fall campaign.

I never felt my calf muscle actually tear during the race that evening. In fact, I performed very well. In what is a common occurrence for most runners who suffer injuries, I didn't notice the problem until after the run that caused it. In my instance, it wasn't until I went out on a run the next day that I felt the pain in my calf. Others sometime feel the pain later that same day, or the next morning when they wake up.

My other injury also occurred while training the summer before the cross country season prior to my senior year. This time the problem was with my right knee, but it was not as serious as the first injury. I experienced a nagging soreness underneath the knee cap. Fortunately, I only had to ease up on my training for a few weeks, and was at full strength for most of my final cross country season.

In the case of both injuries, I stopped running as soon as I felt pain. Listening to your body can be the best preventive medicine. It's important to respond properly to the stress signals your body sends out. It's not always easy. A fine line often exists between the occasional aches and pains all runners experience from time to time and the more persistent pains that may signal serious injuries. You can run with minor aches, but not with a sustained feeling of pain.

Minor aches and tightness in your muscles will begin to subside as you get further into a run. Pain that results from an injury only gets worse the longer you go. This is the most obvious way to determine whether what you are feeling on any particular run is worth worrying about. If it gets worse — stop. If it lessens — complete the entire run. If it remains a minor annoyance — shorten the run. Don't ever hesitate taking a day or two off if you're in doubt about whether the soreness you feel might have harmful consequences.

Obviously, you're in trouble if you feel discomfort in one specific area when just walking. Don't even try to run that day. I'm not talking about a general feeling of tightness in your legs the day after a hard run. That's common and should not cause concern. It's a problem when one specific part of your body feels a whole lot worse than the rest.

TYPES OF INJURIES

Runners usually develop injuries in the **knee** and **shin**. Other problem areas include the calf muscle, Achilles tendon, hamstring muscle, hip, back and the arch of the foot.

It's a rare occurrence for any runner to train for years on end without experiencing some degree of knee trouble. The most frequent injury is aptly named **runner's knee**. The medical term for it is *chondromalacia patella*. You might be suffering from it if you are feeling pain underneath or around your knee cap. It's caused by your knee cap becoming misaligned. This makes it rub up against the surrounding cartilage. As you might expect, this causes pain and swelling in the knee area.

I suffered this injury during my early running days in high school. My problem was similar to that which many other runners experience in their teens: my bones were growing at a faster rate than my muscles and tendons. Besides adolescent growth spurts, major causes of runner's knee include weak quadricep muscles, frequent downhill running and serious pronation (over-pronation, common among runners with flat feet, occurs when the pressure from striking on the heel of the foot causes the legs to rotate inward, which puts added pressure on the kneecap).

Most of us experience shin pain or **shin splints** at some point during our running careers. It happens to runners at all levels. Shin splints are caused by running on hard surfaces which inflame muscle fibers attached to the shin bone. Pain is felt along parts of, or in many instances, the entire shin area from above the ankle to below the knee. The pain is usually more severe at the beginning of a run. New runners are especially susceptible because of the unfamiliar stress they are placing on their lower legs. Running in worn out shoes is also a frequent cause of shin splints. Many advanced runners develop shin splints from increasing their mileage dramatically.

Most runners are able to train through mild cases of shin splints. In these instances, the body is able to adapt to the added stress and the pain recedes over time. But if the pain persists, do not try to run through it. If left untreated, a serious case of shin splints can lead to a stress fracture in your lower leg.

The Achilles tendon is the large tendon connecting the two major calf muscles to the back of the heel bone. Under too much stress, the tendon tightens, causing it to become inflamed. If left untreated, a layer of scar tissue, which is less flexible than the tendon, may appear. This increases the risk of a tear or rupture of the tendon. Fortunately, for most runners, it rarely advances beyond the inflammation stage.

The culprit in most cases is the calf muscles. Calf muscles that are over-worked or tight exert added pressure on the tendon. Problems associated with the calf frequently result from overtraining or a lack of stretching. Excessive hill training and inflexible running shoes can also cause inflammation of the Achilles tendon.

TREATING INJURIES

Why do many people assume that serious runners automatically qualify as experts in sports medicine? The topic I am most frequently asked about by friends who run is not recommended training schedules or racing tips; it's injuries.

A typical question is: "Matt, I've been experiencing pain in my right knee while running. What is it? And how can I get rid of it?" I usually offer them some general advice about icing and taking it easy for a while, and if that doesn't work, to consult a sports physician. But I also make it clear to them that I'm no expert when it comes to diagnosing and treating injuries. But there are plenty of qualified sports medical experts who can provide more assistance.

INJURIES: WHO TO CALL & WHAT TO DO

*The **American Running and Fitness Association**, a nonprofit educational association dedicated to the promotion of aerobic exercise, has a nationwide listing of sports medicine specialists. Their referral service number is 800-776-2732.*

*They also offer some treatment tips. At the top of their list of treatments for knee and shin injuries are **ice** and **rest**. Ice the affected area for 10-15 minutes, 2-3 times a day. Stop running until the pain is gone, or until you are able to run without having to alter your normal running motion.*

Exercises that strengthen muscles in the affected area or the area surrounding it can also get you back on the roads and trails quicker. Leg extensions, with or without weights, strengthen your quadriceps muscle. Stronger quadriceps serve to stabilize your kneecap, which enables you to recover from runner's knee. I did weeks of negative resistance exercises with weights to rehabilitate my torn calf muscle. Strengthening the muscles and tendons in the front part of the leg lowers the risk of shin splints. A simple exercise using an ankle weight strapped to your foot is one way to both stretch and strengthen the area. Sitting on a chair, move your foot up and down from the ankle without bending the knee.

Treat back pain seriously. Stop running and consult a doctor if you suffer any symptoms beyond mild levels of pain or irritation. I've seen friends' running days come to an end because they did not treat their back pain soon enough. If you are experiencing mild pain and still want to run, stay away from hills. Hill running, both up and down, puts tremendous pressure on your back.

Other treatment suggestions include: taking aspirin or ibuprofen to reduce inflammation, applying compression in the form of wraps or compresses to the affected area, elevating the affected area and applying heat after the swelling and pain has subsided. Consult a doctor if these treatment recommendations don't eliminate the pain, and certainly before taking any medication — including aspirin or ibuprofen — on a regular basis.

WAYS TO AVOID INJURIES
Don't Over-Train
Many running injuries are caused by over-training. Avoid dramatically increasing your weekly mileage over a short time span. Limit your increases to no more than ten percent a week. If you change your running routine in any manner, such as varying the terrain, taking time off, or purchasing new shoes, cut back on your mileage by about 10 percent for a week to give your body an opportunity to accommodate the changes. Also, try not to get too preoccupied with hitting a specific mileage target for each week. Listen to your body.

Another important point, one which I have stressed throughout this book, is varying the intensity of your workouts. Remember to take it easy at the very beginning and end of every run. Always follow a long run, speed workout, or race with an easy run.

Finally, for all of you competitive types, don't over-race. One marathon, two at the most, is enough in a year. 10-K enthusiasts shouldn't usually go beyond racing competitively twice a month.

Vary the Terrain & Surface That You Run On

Alternating between dirt and asphalt surfaces, hilly and flat terrains will more evenly distribute the strain on your muscles. "The body tolerates variety better than constant repetition," according to Dr. Stan James, a Eugene, Oregon orthopedist used by Olympic marathon champion Joan Benoit Samuelson. Wherever possible, try to stay off sidewalks. Most sidewalks are made out of concrete, which are harder than streets made of asphalt. If you have no alternative to a hard surface, choose the street over the sidewalk in areas where traffic is not a problem. Sidewalks are also frequently cracked and uneven.

Probably the best place to run is on a dirt path. They offer the best combination of stability and cushioning to your feet and legs. As a bonus, they also offer the best scenery. Running on grass is not a bad alternative, but it usually does not offer the sure-footedness of a dirt trail. The uneven nature of grassy areas and beaches forces the muscles and tendons in your legs to work harder than on flat surfaces, increasing the risk of injury.

Running on beaches is generally not a good idea. The combination of a natural slope and soft sand results in uneven footing. If you are inclined to run on the beach, do so at low tide when you are more likely to find a level surface and packed sand close to the water line.

Take it easy going downhill. It's fine to try to make up for lost time on a downhill during a race, but it's counterproductive during your routine training runs. When running downhill, the force on the kneecap is five times your body weight, compared to 1.8 times your body weight on level ground and 3.5 times heading uphill.

Rest & Stretching

Always try to get a sufficient amount of sleep on a consistent basis. Try not to dip under 7-8 hours of sleep a night under normal training circumstances. Those engaged in marathon training, or frequent 10-K racing, should increase their amount of sleep by another hour. There's no better way to avoid getting stuck with one of those stubborn colds, which can set back your training a week or two, than consistently getting in a good night's sleep.

It's always a good idea to give yourself a day or two off from running each week. This gives you the opportunity to completely rest the muscles you use for running. It also offers you the chance to play another sport. Remember, diversity is the spice of life. Many runners erroneously believe their level of fitness will decline if they take a day or two off a week. Numerous studies have concluded that resting helps rather than hampers your running performance.

The average runner should stretch at least ten minutes before and after a run. The American Running and Fitness Association says: "Running has many benefits, but improving flexibility is not one of them. Running strengthens leg muscles, but it also shortens and tightens them. Tight muscles and tendons hurt your form, and poor running form leads to injuries."

Studies have shown that warm tissue stretches better than cold tissue. But this should not be used as an excuse to neglect stretching before a run in favor of only doing it after warming up or completing a run. Muscles, tendons and ligaments are more prone to injuries that are cold and tight.

Stretches should **not** be forced. Think about exhaling as you begin a stretch in order to remain relaxed. Here are a few basic recommended stretches to do before and after running:

• **Wall Pushup**: This benefits the calf muscle. Stand a few feet from a wall, lean inwards until you feel the strain in your calf, keeping your legs straight and knees locked. Hold this position for about 10 seconds. Repeat the process holding the same position with one leg, while moving the other leg closer to the wall with the knee bent.

A slight variation of this stretch is called the **Wall Lean** and benefits the shin and Achilles tendon. For this stretch, you are allowed to bend both of your knees while leaning inward against a wall, with one leg closer to the wall than the other.

Another easy way to stretch the Achilles is the **heel drop**. Stand on the balls of your feet on a curb or stairs with your legs straight and drop both heels down and hold for 10 seconds. Repeat the stretch 5- 7 times. A simple way to strengthen the calf muscles is to do toe raises

• **Foot Lift**: This benefits the quadriceps muscle. Stand on one foot, holding onto something for support, and grab your other ankle, pulling the leg up back until your heel touches your backside. Hold for about 20 seconds. Repeat with your other leg.

• **Hamstring Stretch**: Obviously, this benefits the hamstring. Put your leg with the knee locked on a chair or table (anything that is a little below waist level). The other leg should remain straight with the knee locked. Bring your head toward the knee of the extended leg until you feel the strain. Hold the position for about 10 seconds. Repeat the process with the other leg.

There are many other stretches that benefit the groin, back, and upper body you may want to do. I realize that many runners refuse to put much effort into stretching. I know, I'm one of them. At a minimum, stretch after a run and focus on loosening up your calf and hamstring muscles.

Running Shoes

Last, but not least, always remember to replace worn out running shoes. Continuing to run in ragged shoes is one of the leading causes of minor injuries (which frequently turn into more serious ones) among runners. Turn to the running shoes section of Chapter 3, *Weather & Running Attire*, for more details.

CHILDREN & INJURIES

Parents should discourage their children from specializing in only one sport at an early age. Recently, this has become a problem, especially with soccer. Children are playing in leagues throughout the entire year. In the case of running, many kids in their early and mid-teens are also now training in all four seasons. This over-emphasis increases the risk of both physical injury and mental burnout.

A recent study of youths across the country found that 75 percent of those involved in a particular sport dropped it by the time they turned 15. Most of the kids did not take up any alternative sport. The best bet for reducing the risk of turning your kids into channel surfing couch potato teens is to encourage them to have fun by enjoying a wide range of athletic activities.

11. CROSS TRAINING

The idea behind cross training is to give yourself the opportunity to take a break from running from time to time in order to enjoy other athletic activities.

WHY CROSS TRAIN?

Cross training offers important physiological and psychological benefits. On the physical side, cross training develops the muscles not used when running. At the same time, muscles used when running are given a chance to rest, thus minimizing the risk of injury.

The psychological gains are just as significant. Cross training serves to sustain your enthusiasm about running. "The best way to stay refreshed and motivated is to cross train at least one day a week," says Steven Ungerleider, Ph.D., a research psychologist in Eugene, Oregon, who serves on the U.S. Olympic Committee.

Cross training balances the use of your muscles, something that cannot be achieved just by running. You're less likely to suffer an injury caused by the overuse of a particular muscle or tendon if you involve more muscles in your training program. Unfortunately, injuries are almost an unavoidable aspect of the sport of running.

Many runners, myself included, suffer from serious bouts of emotional distress when injured. Cross training helps divert your attention away from the injury. By participating in other sports, you're able to relieve some of those fitness withdrawal symptoms.

WEIGHT TRAINING

Weight training can serve as a good complement to running. If you have limited experience with weights, or have back problems, you might want to consult a doctor before starting weight training.

I recommend concentrating only on your upper body. Running itself offers enough of a workout for your legs. The jury is still out on whether a rigorous weight training routine for your legs does more harm than good. Lifting weights develops your leg muscles in a manner different from the type of strengthening that occurs more naturally from running. It also puts unwarranted stress on the ligaments, tendons, and muscles of your legs, especially in the area surrounding the knee.

Generally, it is wise to only use weights on your legs when it is recommended by a physical therapist or sports doctor as a rehabilitation exercise when recovering from an injury (or in the case of an adolescent child when growth spurts leave them with periods of uneven muscle development). In these cases, the weight training usually will supplant rather than act as a supplement to your running schedule.

Try and find some extra time during the week to work on your upper body strength. You only have to set aside as little as 30 minutes two or three times a week to achieve positive results. The best time to lift is either on a day off or after one of your easier runs. I prefer to lift after I run rather than before. I find it's better to hit the weights when I am loosened up after my run, rather than hitting the pavement when I am tight from lifting. But the order in which you do the two workouts is not crucial.

Why Lift Weights?

Lifting weights can bolster your running performance for two related reasons. **First**, strengthening the arms, chest and shoulders will improve your running form. Many of you out there run far less efficiently than what you are capable of because your upper body is so much weaker than your legs.

Waist down, the form looks great, but on top the shoulders are crouched in, the chest sunken, and the arms swing all over the place. Lifting can help to get all those upper body parts in sync with those below the belt. It will help to economize the range of motion used by your upper body when you run. This saves precious energy which can be channeled into increasing your pace.

Second, lifting helps to compensate for the burden on your legs as they begin to tire towards the end of a long run or speed workout. The weight training you do really comes in handy towards the end of the race when your legs may begin to cramp up. As your legs — not to mention your stomach and head — start sending you signals that they're starting to finish for the day, you can rely more heavily on the muscles in your upper body to get you through the race. The weight training will halt the slide many runners experience during the final miles, and can save you five to ten minutes in time.

Additional upper body strength will also serve as a valued resource under less severe occasions, such as the end of a long run, a 10-K race, or the last 150 yards of an 800 meter interval. It's the secret weapon, which many of your competitors do not have in their arsenal, that pays dividends at the time when you need them most: when you are pushing your body as far as it will go. I was not blessed with the natural speed many of my college competitors had, so lifting was my way of compensating for it.

You don't have to turn yourself into Arnold Schwartzenegger to benefit from weight-lifting. Carrying that much bulk and drinking all that muscle building protein powder mix would surely detract from your running. Concentrate on three to four exercises two to three days a week that work on your arms, chest and shoulders. The entire workout should last no more than 30 to 40 minutes.

Where Should You Work Out?

The most common place to workout is at a health club. They all have a wide selection of weight-lifting devices, including nautilus machines, universal gyms, and free weights. But you do not have to rely on joining a health club, many of which are expensive to join and loaded with many high-tech machines you will never use.

If you have the room to do it at home, go out to a sporting goods store and purchase a weight bench, a few bars, and a bunch of weights. It is a convenient and cheaper alternative to joining a club. Another possibility is finding a nearby community center. It doesn't have to be fancy. All you really need is either a universal gym set-up or free weights and a bench. Sometimes Y's, schools, or hotels offer access to their weight rooms at rates far less than what a commercial health club charges.

Basic Exercises

The three basic exercises you'll want to do are the bench press, the military press and curls. The bench press works the chest, military the shoulders and curls the arms. Out of the three, curls are the least important, since you are still working out your arms to some extent in the other exercises. So leave the curls for the end of the workout.

The **bench press** involves lying on your back on a bench that holds a bar with weights in place above your head. On a universal machine, the bench is separated from the weights and bar, but the positioning of the bar remains the same. Raise the bar up until your arms are completely extended. The length of the bar should be positioned directly above the upper part of your chest, just below your shoulders. Bring the bar down and back up slowly. Repeat the process until you have done 10 to 12 repetitions. Take about a two minute rest and then repeat the exercise two to three more times.

For runners new to weight training, start off with light weights. In the case of the bench press, don't go much beyond fifty percent of your body weight. Women may want to start out at 35-40 percent of body weight. As time goes on and the reps start getting easier, increase the weight five to ten pounds.

The **military press** you do sitting down on a bench (free weights), stool (universal), or chair connected to the machine (nautilus). You raise a bar, aligned with your shoulders, slowly above your head until your arms are completely extended and then bring it back down to shoulder length. Like the bench press and the curls, repeat the process until you have done 10-12 reps, rest a couple of minutes, and do another two to three sets.

You will find that raising weights above your head sitting down is a lot more difficult to do then raising weights above your chest lying down. For the military press, start out lifting only a bit more than half of the weight you are using for the bench press. The military press puts a significant amount of pressure on your lower back. If you suffer from back problems, consult a doctor before attempting to do this exercise. For those who don't suffer from back problems, it's still a good idea to use a weight belt, which adds support to your back, while doing the military press. You may look silly, but it really helps to shore up your back.

Finally, it is time for the **curls**, which will strengthen your biceps. These can be done using a bar with weights, a barbell, or on a nautilus or universal machine. Stand holding the weights with your arms fully extended downwards. Keep your elbows in place at the sides of your body and lift the weights up until the top of your forearm is almost parallel with your shoulders. Remember to keep your back straight while you are lifting the weights up. Do 10-12 reps, and a total of three sets. In terms of weight, choose whatever feels comfortable to complete 10-12 reps. Relative to benching and the military press, curls involves the least amount of weights.

If you find that your daily schedule doesn't allow enough time to include weight training, that's okay. Don't compromise your planned running schedule in order to keep up with lifting. Remember the whole purpose behind lifting is to use it as a vehicle for improving your running performance, not to limit it. If you find that you do not have the time for both, stop the lifting. Another possibility is to buy barbells, which are easy to store, and do the lifts described above with less weight and without a bench. The return will not be as high, but you will still benefit from the workouts.

EXERCISE MACHINES
For those who like indoor alternatives to running there are many exercise machines to choose from. Some of the most popular ones are machines that duplicate the motions of cross country skiing,

stationary bikes, rowing machines, and treadmills. Recent studies have revealed that the cardiovascular benefits of using a stationary bike come close to matching running. Exercise machines are widely available in health clubs or may be purchased for home use.

A recent review of exercise machines in the magazine *Runner's World* gave high marks to the NordicTrack, the Concept II Rowing Ergometer rowing machine, the Sportech treadmill, and the Schwinn Airdyne stationary bike. All these machines have been on the market for over a decade and continue to be popular items to buy. They range in price from $400 to over $2000, with the bottom of the line NordicTrack and the Schwinn Airdyne the cheapest alternatives, and the Sportech treadmill and the top of the line NordicTrack models at the high end.

WINTER OUTDOOR SPORTS

In my view, there's nothing more refreshing than doing something that warms up your body in the cool brisk air. That's why I enjoy running so much during the winter months. There are a few other outdoor sports suited to the winter climate that offer an excellent workout. Ice skating is a good way to work your quadriceps and hamstring muscles while also obtaining a modest aerobic workout. Plus it's cheap. Downhill skiing takes a bit more skill and money, but it's a terrific workout for all your upper leg and back muscles. It also provides a modest aerobic workout.

Cross country skiing provides an excellent aerobic workout. It's far cheaper and easier to master than downhill skiing, and much more accessible. I've been cross country skiing for years and love it. It's a superb alternative to fighting the ice and snow in a pair of running shoes.

SWIMMING & POOL RUNNING

Swimming offers the opportunity to get a first rate aerobic workout without stress on your legs muscles from the impact of striking the ground. The truly dedicated runner might want to consider buying a buoyant vest and jumping in a pool from time to time. Some runners use deep water running as part of their rehabilitation program when recovering from serious injuries. Others use it as part of their routine training since if offers an aerobic workout comparable to running without the impact on leg muscles.

A PLUG FOR SOCCER

Many of the top international marathoners were first soccer players. An hour of soccer, with its varied periods of jogging and sprinting, includes most of the ingredients of an enduring interval workout. It offers runners one the best alternative workouts compared to any other popular team sport.

12. DIET

I've never been a big proponent of placing undue emphasis on what you eat while training. This may be a contrarian point of view, but I subscribe to the belief that the positive health benefits from maintaining a consistent running schedule far outweigh any of the negatives acquired from putting down an occasional Big Mac and fries or a juicy steak. In my view, all the hard training entitles you to indulge more often in less than nutritious food groups than the average person.

THE IMPORTANCE OF CARBOHYDRATES

Many sports dieticians stress the benefits to athletes of diets high in **carbohydrates** and low in fat – although some recent studies have shown that diets high in carbohydrates only benefit runners who train at moderate levels, not high levels. During intense physical activities, such as running a hard 10-K, your body relies more heavily on burning off carbohydrates relative to fat. Carbohydrates supply you with energy at a lower oxygen level than fats. Therefore, burning off fat requires you to use more of your precious oxygen supply while you are running.

The increased intake of carbohydrates is also known to raise your **glycogen** level. Glycogen is a form of energy stored in your muscles that is used while running. It's important to eat foods high in carbohydrates soon after running to ensure that depleted levels of glycogen are replaced as soon as possible.

Foods high in carbohydrates include: cereals, bagels, breads, pasta, fruit and fish. There are numerous ways that you can increase the amount of carbohydrates in your diet relative to fat. Drink skim milk over whole milk and reduce your use of butter. Try to replace high fat animal proteins with low fat vegetarian sources such as beans. Of course, eating more vegetables and fruit is always a good thing. Many of them are rich in Vitamin C, enhancing iron absorption.

FAT

Diets with a significant **fat** content may not be a problem for some athletes. Highly trained athletes can burn off fat more efficiently than normal individuals. High fat diets may not have a detrimental effect on cholesterol levels in the case of well-trained athletes. According to Dr. John Laddy, associate director of sports medicine at the University of New York at Buffalo, cholesterol levels are not affected because high intensity runners burn fat almost as soon as they consume it, so the fat doesn't have a chance to clog their arteries.

Fat also serves as a fuel for exercising muscles. Fat cells are found within muscle fibers, although, as mentioned earlier, they do not burn as efficiently as carbohydrates when exercising. But for those involved in high endurance pursuits, such as running a marathon, your body needs both carbohydrates and fats.

Heavy duty marathon training increases the potential for muscle tissue loss and a drop in body weight. A diet that includes a moderate level of fats helps to restore lost muscle tissue and maintain your body weight. The popular pursuit of *carbo-loading* prior to a marathon can help only so much. Your body can store only enough carbohydrates for 90 minutes of exercise.

Healthy high fat foods include: peanut butter, mayonnaise, olive oil and milk. Also, it's a good idea to keep in mind that dark colored meats such as tuna, chicken thighs, trout, and beef contain more iron and zinc than light colored meats. So red meat can't be all that bad!

I'm also happy to report that recent studies have shown that drinking a moderate amount of alcohol is also okay ("moderate" translates into about a drink a day.) Wine is thought to be the best choice. It's known to prevent bad LDL cholesterol from getting stuck on your artery walls. Too much alcohol, however, can negatively affect your ability to metabolize carbohydrates and can lead to water loss.

In the final analysis, it's still unclear how much more effective high carbohydrate diets are for runners. For high intensity training, it may not make any difference at all. This isn't to suggest that everyone should partake in a diet high in fat. Studies have shown a clear link between diets high in fat, especially saturated fats, and heart disease and other health problems. The proportion of carbohydrates to fats in a diet probably matters more for lower- to mid-level intensity runners than the more advanced crowd.

All runners should avoid any type of crash dieting. Low-calorie diets often lack sufficient calcium, which can lead to bone loss. Also, as discussed previously, it's vital to replace all the calories you lose from running in order to maintain muscle fiber. In most cases, it's more important to maintain a healthy appetite than worrying too much about how healthy your diet is. Runners with exceedingly bad eating habits can still eat everything they want. They should, however, make an attempt to demonstrate some common sense with regard to their diet.

13. RUNNING CLUBS

I'm a big proponent of joining a running club. Since graduating from college, I've been a member of running clubs in Cambridge MA, and in Washington D.C., where I currently reside. For competitive runners, the clubs offer the opportunity to get together regularly with other serious runners for speed workouts or long hard runs. Many of these clubs organize group runs on a frequent basis which help runners of all levels stay motivated.

Running clubs also offer an important safety benefit to women. You can find running partners of similar ability to train with and thus avoid having to run alone. Clubs offer all runners a great social outlet for making new friends who are guaranteed to share at least one important interest. Finally, when traveling, running clubs are a great resource for local information on good places to run.

Listed below are some of the larger running clubs located in major cities across the United States. The list was provided by the Road Runners Club of America (RCAA). The Road Runners Club of America is the national association of not-for-profit running clubs, dedicated to promoting long distance running as a competitive sport and as healthful exercise. Founded in 1958, they now have over 530 grassroots running clubs all over the United States and Guam.

For information on how to find a club, or to start a club, or general information on running, you can contact the RRCA at (703) 836-0558.

Annapolis, MD
Annapolis Striders, 706 members
Contact: Matthew Mace (410) 647-7633h (410) 347-7690

Atlanta, GA
Atlanta Track Club 10,712 members
Contact: Julie Emmons (404) 872-0808h (404) 231-9065w

Baltimore, MD
Baltimore Road Runners Club, 952 members
Contact: Robert T. Hall (410) 661-5725h (410) 243-3153w

Beaverton, OR
Oregon Road Runners Club, 1,807 members
Contact: Gordon Lovie (503) 646-7867w

Bellbrook, OH
Ohio River Road Runners Club, 910 members
Contact: Bill Mercer (513) 848-2576h (513) 455-7209w

Birmingham, AL
Birmingham Track Club, 973 members
Contact: Norman Thomas (205) 290-0223h (205) 977-7934w

Boston, MA
Boston Running Club, 264 members
Contact: Page Martini (617) 964-7802w

Charleston, SC
Charleston Running Club, 290 members
Contact: Jim Renneker (803) 720-8859h

Chesapeake, VA
Tidewater Striders, 1,354 members
Contact: R.P. Kale (804) 471-2228h

Clinton, MS
Mississippi Track Club, 699 members
Contact: Bob Coleman (601) 856-9884h (601) 965-5268w

Colorado Springs, CO
Pikes Peak Road Runners, 932 members
Contact: Patricia Lockhart (719) 598-2953h (719) 632-9100w

Dallas, TX
Cross Country Club of Dallas, 1,376 members
Contact: Cricket Griffin (214) 750-5871h (214) 855-6263w

Davenport, IA
Cornbelt Running Club, 1,717 members
Contact: Bill Teubel (319) 285-4128h

Detroit, MI
Motor City Striders, 1,114 members
Contact: Dr. Edward Kozloff (810) 544-9099h

Denver, CO
Rocky Mountain RRC, 616 members
Contact: Bill Carey (303) 987-8856h (303) 239-3722w

Hartford, CT
Hartford Track Club, Inc., 360 members
Contact: J. Braun (203) 228-4252h (203) 584-7336

Honolulu, HI
Mid-Pacific RRC, 415 members
Contact: Robert Doleman (808) 833-7803h (808) 438-2255w

Houston, TX
Houston Area Road Runners Assoc., 1,203 members
Contact: Joy Smith (713) 265-3116h

Huntsville, AL
Huntsville Track Club, 656 members
Contact: Harold Tinsley (205) 881-9077h (205) 882-4572w

Indianapolis, IN
Indy Runners Inc., 1,029 members
Contact: Kevin J. Caraher (317) 290-1737h (317) 635-9788w

Jacksonville, FL
Jacksonville Track Club, 780 members
Contact: John Tenbroeck (904) 387-0528h (904) 384-8725w

Knoxville, TN
Knoxville Track Club, 987 members
Contact: Brint Adams (615) 966-4189h (615) 584-3377w

Madison, WI
Wisconsin Track Club, 96 members
Contact: Eric Stabb (608) 255-9398

Memphis, TN
Memphis Runners Track Club, 1,550 members
Contact: Paul L. Ireland (901) 388-5009h (901) 528-4224w

Miami, FL
Miami Runners, 1,863 member
Contact: Jorge Blanco (305) 227-1500w

Milwaukee, WI
Badgerland Striders, 1,215 members
Contact: Glenn Wargolet (414) 352-2168h

Nashua, NH
Gate City Striders, 322 members
Contact: Steve Doyle (603) 889-5528h

Nashville, TN
Nashville Striders, Inc., 875 members
Contact: Kibby Clayton (615) 353-0808h (615) 353-0822w

New Orleans, LA
New Orleans Track Club, 1,580 members
Contact: Chuck George (504) 468-1488h (504) 482-6682w

New York, NY
New York Road Runners Club, 29,000 members
Contacts: Allan Steinfeld (212) 860-4455

Philadelphia, PA
Northeast Roadrunners of Philadelphia, 209 member
Contact: Gerald J. Nolan (215) 535-7335h

Portland, ME
Maine Track Club 360 members
Contact: Ron Pelton (207) 846-9039h

Raleigh, NC
North Carolina Roadrunners, 517 members
Contact: Jim Young (919) 231-0714

Raymore, MO
Mid-America Running Association, 1,171 members
Contact: Karen Raymer (816) 331-4286

Rockville, MD
Montgomery County RRC, 1,348 members
Contact: Phil Quinn (301) 977-7361h

Sacramento, CA
Buffalo Chips Running Club, 569 members
Contact: Stephen Topper (916) 424-3454h (916) 374-5869w

St. Louis, MO
St. Louis Track Club, 1,047 members
Contact: Tom Eckelman (314) 781-3926w

St. Paul, MN
Northern Lights Running Club, 210 members
Contact: Sue Wurl (612) 487-1947h (612) 653-2946w

San Antonio, TX
San Antonio Roadrunners, 750 members
Contact: John Delgado (210) 648-4729h (210) 532-5158w

San Francisco, CA
Dolphin South End Runners Club, 444 members
Contact: Joe Oakes (415) 903-0341h

Santa Fe, NM
Santa Fe Striders, 77 members
Contact: John Pollak (505) 983-2144

Seattle, WA
Seattle Marathon Association, 48 members.
Contact: Rick Johnston (206) 526-7170h (206) 821-6474w

Syracuse, NY
Syracuse Chargers Track Club, 1,133 members
Contact: Dave Oja (315) 446-6285h

Tallahassee, FL
Gulf Winds Track Club, 593 members
Contact: Mae Cleveland (904) 576-0585h

Toledo, OH
Toledo Road Runners Club, 862 members
Contact: Jeff Bertram (419) 534-2151h

Tucson, AZ
Southern Arizona RRC, 888 members
Contact: Robert Tram (520) 318-44762h (602) 326-9383w

Washington, D.C.
D.C. Road Runners, 856 members
Contact: Robert Platt (703) 486-1466h (202) 675-6322

The contact people for these clubs are subject to change. If you are having problems getting in touch with one of these clubs, or would like information on other clubs not included in this list, contact the Road Runners Club of America.

RUNNING TO CURE CANCER!

Across the US in 1996, close to 10,000 members of the Leukemia Society of America's **Team in Training** *program will experience the thrill and sense of accomplishment that comes from having completed a marathon. They will also discover the deep personal satsifaction of helping the Leukemia Society find a cure for leukemia, lymphoma, multiple myeloma, and Hodgkin's Disease.*

As a **Team in Training** *member, you'll receive comprehensive training advice from seasoned coaches as well as an all-expenses paid trip to a marathon. While the Leukemia Society will help you reach your personal marathon goals, they ask you to help them raise money to significantly accelerate cures for leukemia and related cancers by the year 2000.*

Each Leukemia Society chapter attends one or more of nearly 40 accredited marathons, including some of the more scenic routes, such as the Bermuda Marathon, Honolulu Marathon, and the Big Sur Marathon. For more information on how to join a **Team in Training** *in your area, call the nationwide toll-free information line at 1/800-955-4572.*

14. YOUR RUNNING LOG

SAMPLE LOG

Day	Temp./Time of Day	Route/Time	Rating/Comments
Sunday	48°/4:30pm	"Bridges"/31:25	5/felt great!
Monday			
Tuesday			
Wednesday			
Thursday			
Friday			
Saturday			

EXPLANATIONS

Give each of your running routes a nickname ("Bridges" in the example above). This offers you a concise way to monitor your progress by comparing the time it takes to run a particular route over several weeks. This is why it's far more useful to record how long you are running rather than the distance.

Rate each of your runs on a 1–5 scale. On your best days, when it all feels so easy from start to finish, give yourself a five. On the really down days, when you're feeling very sluggish, give yourself a one. Most of your runs should eventually receive ratings of three or four, solid but not exceptional. It's also a good idea to jot down a brief comment or two on how you felt during each run. For example, you might comment on whether your legs felt strong or weak, or how you felt overall during different parts of the run.

WEEKLY LOG

Day	Temp./Time of Day	Route/Time	Rating/Comments
Sunday			
Monday			
Tuesday			
Wednesday			
Thursday			
Friday			
Saturday			

Additional Comments:

WEEKLY LOG

Day	Temp./Time of Day	Route/Time	Rating/Comments
Sunday			
Monday			
Tuesday			
Wednesday			
Thursday			
Friday			
Saturday			

Additional Comments:

WEEKLY LOG

Day	Temp./Time of Day	Route/Time	Rating/Comments
Sunday			
Monday			
Tuesday			
Wednesday			
Thursday			
Friday			
Saturday			

Additional Comments:

WEEKLY LOG

Day	Temp./Time of Day	Route/Time	Rating/Comments
Sunday			
Monday			
Tuesday			
Wednesday			
Thursday			
Friday			
Saturday			

Additional Comments:

WEEKLY LOG

Day	Temp./Time of Day	Route/Time	Rating/Comments
Sunday			
Monday			
Tuesday			
Wednesday			
Thursday			
Friday			
Saturday			

Additional Comments:

WEEKLY LOG

Day	Temp./Time of Day	Route/Time	Rating/Comments
Sunday			
Monday			
Tuesday			
Wednesday			
Thursday			
Friday			
Saturday			

Additional Comments:

WEEKLY LOG

Day	Temp./Time of Day	Route/Time	Rating/Comments
Sunday			
Monday			
Tuesday			
Wednesday			
Thursday			
Friday			
Saturday			

Additional Comments:

WEEKLY LOG

Day	Temp./Time of Day	Route/Time	Rating/Comments
Sunday			
Monday			
Tuesday			
Wednesday			
Thursday			
Friday			
Saturday			

Additional Comments:

To order more copies of **THE SMART RUNNER'S HANDBOOK** ($9.95), or any of our golf or travel guides, please order from:

Open Road Publishing
P.O. Box 20226
Columbus Circle Station
New York, NY 10023

Tell us how many copies you want, and please remember: you <u>must</u> include the price of each book **plus shipping and handling charges** with your order. *Shipping and handling is $3.00 for the first book, and $1.00 for each additional book.*

Open Road also offers significant discounts for quantity purchases.